A SAINSBU

T

VEGE

GOURMET

MEALS FOR ENTERTAINING AND SPECIAL OCCASIONS

ROSAMOND RICHARDSON

Amber J. Rave
1991

CONTENTS

Published exclusively for J Sainsbury plc
Stamford House Stamford Street
London SE1 9LL
by Martin Books
Simon & Schuster Consumer Group
Fitzwilliam House 32 Trumpington Street
Cambridge CB2 1QY

ISBN 0 85941 540 6

First published 1985
Fifth impression 1991

Printed in Great Britain

THE AUTHOR

Rosamond Richardson is the author of several books, including the highly successful Sainsbury cookbook *Vegetarian Meals*. She was presenter of BBC TV's 'Discovering Patchwork' and co-presenter of BBC TV's 'Discovering Hedgerows', and has also done a short cookery series for BBC East and a series on the uses of herbs for Anglia Television. She has been a regular contributor to BBC Radio Cambridgeshire. As well as publications to accompany her television series, her books include *Hedgerow Cookery, Cooking for Kids, The Little Garlic Book, The Little Mushroom Book, The Little Nut Book, Memorable Meals in Minutes* and *Roses, a Celebration*.

Rosamond has three children and lives in a small Essex village.

INTRODUCTION

There are, I have discovered, great rewards to entertaining with vegetarian food – by which I mean dishes that do not contain any meat or meat products. The food is delicious, visually attractive and very satisfying. I have tried in this book to produce a delicate, delectable style of vegetarian cooking for an elegant way of eating. Certainly no heavy 'veggie' label is necessary for this type of cookery – the nut cutlet is a thing of the past! Many people treated to such fare simply will not notice that it is meatless, and will feel as satisfied – or even more so – as they would be by a more traditional meal.

Another bonus with this type of food is that it is very healthy. The recipes in this book are not only nutritious but are often low in fats and sugars and high in fibre. A further advantage is that, for the same effort, you can produce a fine

Dinner Party Menu 8 (page 94)

meal at a far lower cost than usual without it being at all apparent, for the food's handsome looks belie its economy.

This style of eating is becoming so popular that the idea of entertaining with vegetarian food is no longer unusual. People are now aware of its delicious possibilities and its exciting versatility. It is indeed exciting to explore the delightful variety of tastes which lie within the alluring spread of ingredients available to us today. A veritable kaleidoscope of vegetables of all flavours and textures are to be found on the shop shelves, not only delicious but a feast for the eye – the glow of peppers, the rich gloss of an aubergine, the lovely range of leaf vegetables from pale to deep green and the oranges and scarlets of tomatoes, carrots and pumpkins – to name but a few. Basics such as rice, pasta, cheese and eggs can be transformed with subtle spices, mixed with colourful vegetables and flavoured with the wide range of fresh green herbs at our

disposal. To an artistic cook who enjoys cooking for special occasions, this offers a challenge of endless variety and pleasure.

The recipes in this book, ranging from hors d'oeuvres, appetisers and soups to main courses, side vegetables and salads, make food look beautiful. Whether for a hot meal or for a cold buffet, there are sights to satisfy the proudest cook. You can experiment with garnishes, such as artistically carved radishes and spring onions, or even decorate your dishes with flowers. Often done in the old days, it seems a pity that we have lost this charming habit – a dash of floral colour can make all the difference to the look of a dish.

Some of the greatest cuisines in the world excel in vegetarian dishes, and we have much to learn from them. Traditional recipes from China, Malaysia and India in particular include creations based around fresh vegetables, fruits, rice, eggs, herbs and spices, and inspire us to experiment. These tastes and combinations were recently a mystery to the European cook, but now, with the supermarket revolution of the past few years, the ingredients are there on the shelves for us to pick up. We can discover for ourselves oriental ways of cooking and adapt them to our tastes – a kind of Western translation.

Experiment with your gourmet vegetarian entertaining – as well as the traditional three-course meal you could try the Eastern idea of offering several dishes at a time on the table, tasting small portions of each to balance their distinctive and individual flavours. A typical Thai feast, for example, is laid out in a decorative pattern of which the rice is the central dish. Around this, placed in a circle, are a soup, a curried dish, a salad, a sauce, a steamed dish and a fried dish. You are invited to make your own combinations on your plate, and eat according to your needs. This idea, which can of course encompass all kinds of variations, makes for a beautifully relaxed way of eating, particularly for the host, who will probably want to sit back

Note on recipes
Ingredients in the recipes are given in both imperial (oz, fl oz, etc.) and metric (g, ml, etc.) measures. Use either set of quantities, but not a mixture of both, in any one recipe. All spoon measures are level spoons unless otherwise stated (metric spoon measures are always level). Egg size, where not specified, is medium (size 3). Preparation and cooking times are given as a guideline: all timings are approximate.

and enjoy the party if he or she has prepared all the food. It is a wonderful way to sample and celebrate the fruits of the earth, both for their gastronomic potential and also for their loveliness in colour, texture and aroma.

Alternatives for strict vegetarians

Those who prefer not to use any animal products in their cooking may find the following alternatives for ingredients useful.

GELATINE

A substitute such as agar-agar, which is available from specialist health food shops, may be used in recipes which call for gelatine-based products, such as Jellied Tomato Ring (page 36).

PUFF PASTRY

A chilled puff pastry which does not contain animal fats is available from most branches of Sainsbury's.

CHEESE

A vegetarian Cheddar cheese is available from most branches of Sainsbury's.

CREAM

A non-dairy cream made with refined vegetable oil is available from most branches of Sainsbury's.

POTTED CHEESE WITH HERBS

Preparation time 20 minutes + chilling | Serves 6

8 oz (225 g) Cheddar cheese, grated finely

2 oz (50 g) sunflower margarine

2 tablespoons (2 × 15 ml spoon) sherry or white wine

2 teaspoons (2 × 5 ml spoon) dried mace

2 tablespoons (2 × 15 ml spoon) mixed fresh herbs, such as thyme, parsley, chives and tarragon, all chopped finely

You can make these cocktail snacks well in advance and keep them in the refrigerator until you need them. Fresh herbs add an aromatic touch of elegance to the cheese.

Mix the finely grated cheese with the margarine in a bowl. Add the sherry or wine and the mace. Mix thoroughly and chill. Shape into little balls and coat with the finely chopped herbs. Serve chilled, on cocktail sticks.

Potted Cheese with Herbs

FRIED INDIAN MIX

Preparation time 20 minutes — Serves 4–6

4 tablespoons (4 × 15 ml spoon) vegetable oil

2 teaspoons (2 × 5 ml spoon) garam masala

4 oz (100 g) shelled, unsalted peanuts

2 oz (50 g) sunflower seeds

½ oz (15 g) each of cumin seeds, mustard seeds and poppy seeds

salt

This is fatally more-ish, and I find that my guests descend on it with cries of greedy delight. It makes them thirsty, too, so a dish of this will help to get a party going!

Heat the oil gently in a frying pan with the garam masala, allowing it to infuse for several minutes. Then turn up the heat a little until the oil is quite hot and fry the peanuts and all the seeds together until they are crisp, which will take between 5 and 10 minutes. Shake the pan often to turn them. Drain off the oil and dry the mixture on kitchen paper towelling. Sprinkle with a little salt and store in airtight jars when cool.

SESAME WAFERS

Preparation time 20 minutes + 10–12 minutes baking — Makes 15–20

2 oz (50 g) sesame seeds

1½ oz (40 g) sunflower margarine

3 oz (75 g) plain flour

1 teaspoon (5 ml spoon) dried mace

1 teaspoon (5 ml spoon) baking powder

1 egg

salt

Oven temperatures:
Gas Mark 4/350°F/180°C
Gas Mark 5/375°F/190°C

I find that these wafery biscuits disappear as fast as I produce them – they melt in the mouth and the toasted sesame seeds give them that certain something. They never fail to be popular.

Preheat the oven to the lower setting. Toast the sesame seeds on a baking tray for about 5 minutes until browned, shaking them around from time to time. Take out of the oven and turn it up to the higher setting.

Rub the margarine into the flour and add the mace, baking powder and salt to taste. Mix in the sesame seeds and then beat in the egg. Place in small spoonfuls on a greased baking tray and flatten them down in the middle. Bake for 10–12 minutes until golden. Cool on a rack.

CRISPY-FRIED CHICK-PEAS

Preparation time 8 minutes + soaking overnight — Serves 4

- *4 oz (100 g) chick-peas, soaked overnight*
- *1 tablespoon (15 ml spoon) vegetable oil*
- *approx. 1 tablespoon (15 ml spoon) garam masala*
- *salt*

One of my favourite stand-bys, these crunchy snacks keep for a long time when stored in airtight jars, and are popular with all age groups. They are delicious little nibbles to hand around with drinks.

Drain the soaked chick-peas and dry them thoroughly. Heat the oil in a frying pan until it is very hot and fry the chick-peas until crisp and golden all over, shaking them frequently in the pan. Drain on kitchen paper towelling. Sprinkle with a little garam masala and salt, and when cool store in an airtight jar.

BRIE AND OLIVE SQUARES

Preparation time 25 minutes — Makes 16

- *6 oz (175 g) ripe Brie*
- *5 fl oz (150 ml) carton of natural yogurt*
- *2 oz (50 g) sunflower margarine, melted*
- *6 oz (175 g) black olives, stoned*
- *8 oz (225 g) can of water-chestnuts, diced*

For the crispy squares:

- *4 slices of white bread, with the crusts removed*
- *vegetable oil for frying*

These creamy snacks combine the exotic taste of black olives with one of France's finest cheeses, and the little crunchy dice of water-chestnut give an appetising texture.

Cut the rind off the Brie and blend it in a liquidiser with the yogurt, margarine and olives. Mix in the diced water-chestnuts.

Cut each slice of bread into 4 squares and fry in the oil until golden brown on both sides. Drain on kitchen paper towelling and spread over the Brie and olive mixture.

AVOCADO PÂTÉ

Preparation time 10 minutes + chilling | Serves 4

1 large ripe avocado

12 stuffed green olives

1 medium-size clove of garlic, crushed

salt and pepper

The addition of olives and garlic to this creamy avocado mixture gives it a tang and a bite. Served on fingers of dry toast, it makes a beautiful morsel to go with pre-dinner drinks. Eat within 2–3 hours if possible.

Cut the avocado in half lengthways and scoop out the flesh. Blend in a liquidiser with the olives and garlic, and season to taste. Serve chilled.

Crispy-fried Chick-peas

Stilton and Walnut Bites

Brie and Olive Squares

Crostini Fiorentini

Avocado Pâté

CROSTINI FIORENTINI

Preparation time 25 minutes + 30 minutes baking — Makes 16

1 small aubergine

2 tablespoons (2 × 15 ml spoon) olive oil

1 onion, chopped finely

2 cloves of garlic, crushed

4 oz (100 g) mushrooms, diced

3 oz (75 g) green olives, stoned and chopped

7 oz (200 g) can of tomatoes, drained and chopped

2 teaspoons (2 × 5 ml spoon) mixed dried herbs

2 oz (50 g) mozzarella cheese, cubed small

4 slices of white bread, with the crusts removed

salt and pepper

To garnish:

a few stuffed olives, sliced

Oven temperature:
Gas Mark 3/325°F/170°C

These little triangles (the title means 'little Florence toasts') have an unmistakably Italian flavour and they are a wonderful appetite-whetter.

Preheat the oven and bake the aubergine, whole, for 30 minutes. Cool before scooping out the flesh. Heat the olive oil in a saucepan and cook the onion and the garlic, covered, for 15 minutes until very soft. Add the mushrooms and cook for a further 2 minutes. Stir in the aubergine flesh, olives, tomatoes and herbs, and cook for another 5 minutes. Season to taste and add the mozzarella. Stir well and allow to cool.

Toast the bread and cut each slice into 4 triangles. Spread with the aubergine mixture and serve, garnished with slices of stuffed olive.

STILTON AND WALNUT BITES

Preparation time 15 minutes + chilling — Makes 20

4 oz (100 g) Stilton

2 oz (50 g) walnut pieces

2 tablespoons (2 × 15 ml spoon) walnut or olive oil

These little nibbles are both crunchy and creamy – quite mouth-watering. As they are quite rich, make them small in size since a little goes a long way.

Blend all the ingredients together in a liquidiser so that they are well-blended but the pieces of nut are still big enough to be crunchy. Chill, then roll into little balls and serve on cocktail sticks.

MELON SPEARS

Preparation time 30–40 minutes — Serves 6

6 oz (175 g) honeydew melon

8 sticks of celery, taken from the inner heart

4 oz (100 g) Jarlsberg cheese

4 oz (100 g) seedless grapes or black grapes, halved and de-pipped

8–10 stuffed green olives, sliced

These are light, refreshing nibbles which make a welcome contrast to richer snacks at a drinks party. A slice of olive in each mouthful adds a delicious tang.

Peel and cut the melon into small cubes, or balls if you have a baller. Cut the celery into ½-inch (1 cm) lengths, and the cheese into ½-inch (1 cm) dice. Spear a cube of melon, a piece of celery, a cube of cheese and a grape on to a cocktail stick, and top with a slice of stuffed olive. Repeat until all the ingredients are used up.

DREAMY DIP

Preparation time 15 minutes — Serves 4

3 oz (75 g) cottage cheese

1 tablespoon (15 ml spoon) natural low fat yogurt

1 tablespoon (15 ml spoon) thick Greek yogurt

1 oz (25 g) dry-roasted peanuts

1 clove of garlic, crushed

salt and pepper

A real treat of puréed cottage cheese and yogurt with the crumbly texture of peanuts. Serve with crudités as a tempting appetiser.

Liquidise all the ingredients together, season to taste with salt and pepper and chill. Serve in a bowl in the centre of a platter surrounded by thin sticks of carrot, cucumber, celery and apple.

BLACK BEAN SOUP

Preparation time 1½ hours + soaking overnight — Serves 6

8 oz (225 g) black beans, soaked overnight
2 pints (1.2 litres) water
1 large onion, chopped
4 celery stalks, including the leaves, chopped
a small bunch of fresh herbs, chopped
2 bay leaves
1 large clove of garlic
2 teaspoons (2 × 5 ml spoon) cayenne pepper
6 cloves and 6 peppercorns, tied in a muslin bag
salt

This is a soup for winter, nourishing and sustaining. It has its own spicy heat, the slight bite of cayenne highlighting its earthy flavours. It is marvellous served with a basket of mixed breads – slices of Granary bread, crusty sesame rolls, pitta bread, crusty wholemeal and poppy seed rolls – a delicious meal in itself.

Drain the soaked beans. Put in a pan with the water and all the vegetables, herbs and seasonings and bring to the boil. Boil rapidly for 10 minutes, then simmer for 1¼ hours. Remove the bay leaves and the muslin bag. Liquidise and serve piping hot.

CHILLED WALNUT SOUP

Preparation time 20–30 minutes + chilling | Serves 4

1 oz (25 g) butter

1 medium-size onion, chopped finely

2 sticks of celery, chopped finely

4 oz (100 g) walnut pieces

1¼ pints (750 ml) vegetable stock

5 fl oz (150 ml) carton of single cream

salt and pepper

This cold soup is exquisite in flavour and texture, and is perfect for a summer party or picnic.

Melt the butter in a frying pan and gently cook the onion and celery until soft. Liquidise the walnuts with a little of the stock so that it is smooth but still with some texture, and stir the mixture into the pan. Add the rest of the stock gradually and cook gently for 10–15 minutes. Season to taste and add the cream. Chill.

SHALLOT SOUP WITH CHEESE

Preparation time 25–35 minutes | Serves 4

3 oz (75 g) butter

4 slices of bread

1 lb (450 g) shallots, peeled and sliced

2 tablespoons (2 × 15 ml spoon) plain flour

1½ pints (900 ml) vegetable stock

5 fl oz (150 ml) carton of double cream

2 oz (50 g) Cheddar cheese, grated finely

salt and pepper

Shallots have a flavour distinctly sweeter than that of their sister the onion. Floating a piece of lightly fried bread covered with finely grated cheese in this delicious soup makes it a wonderful starter to a lunch, best followed by a light, salady main course.

Melt 1 oz (25 g) of the butter in a frying pan and lightly fry the slices of bread on both sides. Put to one side on kitchen paper towelling.

Melt the remaining butter and add the shallots. Cook gently for about 10 minutes until softened. Stir in the flour and gradually add the stock. Simmer gently and add the double cream. Season to taste with salt and pepper. Put the slices of bread into four soup bowls and top each one with a quarter of the grated cheese. Pour the soup over the top and serve piping hot.

GARLIC SOUP

Preparation time 40 minutes | Serves 4

16 large cloves of garlic, unpeeled

1½ pints (900 ml) water

1 teaspoon (5 ml spoon) salt

a little black pepper

1 teaspoon (5 ml spoon) mixed dried herbs

2 cloves

4 sprigs of parsley

3 egg yolks

3 tablespoons (3 × 15 ml spoon) olive oil

The subtle, elusive flavour of boiled garlic in this unusual starter is a far cry from the hot taste of uncooked garlic. It is transformed by the cooking process and makes a really delicious soup. Serve it with warm french bread and hand around a bowl of parmesan cheese to sprinkle over the top.

Boil the garlic in the water with the salt, pepper, herbs, cloves and parsley for 30 minutes, covered. Meanwhile beat the egg yolks in a bowl and stir in the olive oil drop by drop, to make a thick mayonnaise base. Beat a little of the hot garlic liquid into the egg mixture, and then, very gradually, strain in the rest through a sieve (pressing the juice out of the garlic cloves with a spoon) and beating all the time. Serve immediately.

CORN CHOWDER

Preparation time 25 minutes | Serves 4

10 oz (335 g) can of sweetcorn, drained

½ pint (300 ml) water

1 oz (25 g) sunflower margarine

6 spring onions, chopped

2 tablespoons (2 × 15 ml spoon) plain flour

½ pint (300 ml) milk

a pinch of cayenne pepper

salt and pepper

To garnish:

chopped parsley

A creamy and scrumptious feast of a soup which makes an excellent lunch served with warm Granary bread and butter. As a starter, it is a party piece – serve it in small bowls and enjoy its radiant colouring.

Empty the can of sweetcorn into a pan and add the water. Bring to the boil and simmer for 10 minutes, then liquidise to a rough purée.

Heat the margarine in a pan and cook the spring onions for a few minutes. Stir in the flour and then, gradually, the milk, stirring until the mixture thickens. Season with the cayenne, salt and pepper. Simmer for 5 minutes and add the sweetcorn purée. Serve sprinkled with the finely chopped parsley.

COLD SPINACH AND LENTIL SOUP

Preparation time 1 hour + a few hours soaking + chilling — Serves 4

- *4 oz (100 g) green lentils, soaked for a few hours*
- *1 lb (450 g) spinach, washed*
- *2 tablespoons (2 × 15 ml spoon) vegetable oil*
- *1 large onion, chopped*
- *1 clove of garlic, chopped*
- *¼ pint (150 ml) water*
- *salt and pepper*

This soup is a rich green colour and gives a touch of splendour to a table laid ready for a party. It is a nourishing, satisfying soup and best served in small quantities if there are other courses to follow. It is lovely hot as well as cold. Serve with a basket of mixed pitta and Granary breads.

Drain the soaked lentils, cover with cold water, bring to the boil and simmer for 40 minutes.

Meanwhile, put the spinach in a saucepan with a little water and salt, bring to the boil and simmer for 6–8 minutes. Drain and chop finely.

Heat the oil in a pan and cook the chopped onion and garlic gently, covered, for 15 minutes until very soft. Stir the spinach and then the onion and garlic into the lentil mixture; add the water and liquidise. Season to taste with salt and pepper and chill until ready to use.

FLORENCE FENNEL SOUP

Preparation time 1 hour — Serves 4

- *2 heads of fennel*
- *1½ oz (40 g) sunflower margarine*
- *2 tablespoons (2 × 15 ml spoon) plain flour*
- *½ pint (300 ml) milk*
- *5 fl oz (150 ml) carton of double cream*
- *1 tablespoon (15 ml spoon) chopped fresh dill weed*
- *salt*

This soup has a sophisticated flavour and is the highlight of any party. It is also quite delicious served on its own with garlic bread for a simple lunch.

Simmer the fennel, whole, in a pan of boiling water for 40 minutes. Meanwhile melt the margarine in a pan, stir in the flour and add the milk gradually, stirring as the sauce thickens. Add the cream and simmer for 10 minutes. Season to taste with a little salt and then purée the fennel with the sauce in a liquidiser. Stir in the chopped dill and serve hot or chilled.

COLD THREE-COLOURED PEPPER SOUP

Preparation time 15 minutes + chilling — Serves 4

- *14 oz (400 g) can of pimentoes, drained*
- *1 pint (600 ml) tomato juice*
- *1 small green pepper, cut into thin strips*
- *1 small yellow pepper, cut into thin strips*
- *salt to taste*

For all its simplicity this is a truly gastronomic soup, ideal for summer parties. Floating strips of green and creamy-yellow peppers in the bright red soup make it a really pretty starter. Serve with Melba toast (see Note below).

Liquidise the pimentoes with the tomato juice, season with a little salt and chill. Garnish the soup decoratively with the strips of green and yellow pepper.

Note: to make Melba toast, slice white bread thinly and cut off the crusts. Place the slices flat on a baking tray and dry out in a very low oven, Gas Mark 2/300°F/150°C, for 1½–2 hours until crisp and golden. Cool on a rack.

Cold Spinach and Lentil Soup

Cold Three-coloured Pepper Soup

Florence Fennel Soup

ROLLED SORREL PANCAKES

Preparation time 40 minutes + 10 minutes baking + standing Serves 4

For the pancakes:

4 oz (100 g) plain flour

¼ pint (150 ml) warm water

3 fl oz (75 ml) milk

2 oz (50 g) margarine, melted

2 eggs

4 oz (100 g) sorrel

½ oz (15 g) grated parmesan cheese

salt

For the filling:

1 lb (450 g) sorrel

8 oz (225 g) curd cheese

salt and pepper

Oven temperature:
Gas Mark 4/350°F/180°C

These little pancake rolls are made with sorrel in the batter, as well as being filled with a delicate sorrel mixture. They make an appetising hors d'oeuvre in the summer months when sorrel is fresh and abundant. Serve with Mushroom Purée (page 30).

Blend the flour with the water, milk, margarine and eggs. Season with salt and leave to stand for an hour. Cook the sorrel with a very little water in a pan until it is a purée. Stir into the batter and mix well.

Lightly grease a frying pan and heat until quite hot. Pour in a little of the batter, spread over and cook for about 1 minute on each side. Repeat to make 12 little pancakes. Preheat the oven.

Wash the sorrel for the filling and cook it in a pan in its own water, stirring constantly until it is a purée. Mix this purée with the curd cheese and season to taste. Spread about 1 tablespoon (15 ml spoon) of this mixture in the centre of each little pancake and roll it up. Place in a baking dish, sprinkle with the parmesan and cook in the oven for 10 minutes.

AUBERGINES PROVENÇALE

Preparation time 45 minutes Serves 4–6

2 medium-size aubergines

4 medium-size courgettes

4 large tomatoes, sliced

1½ oz (40 g) butter

2 cloves of garlic, chopped finely

This dish both looks and tastes seductive – the strong, rustic flavours of peppers, garlic and herbs ally beautifully with the aubergines and courgettes cooked in good olive oil. A princely hors d'oeuvre. It is quite rich, so serve with bread.

Slice the aubergines and the courgettes, about ¼ inch (5 mm) thick. Sprinkle with salt and leave to sweat for half an hour.

Meanwhile, sauté the sliced tomatoes in the

2 tablespoons (2 × 15 ml spoon) finely chopped parsley

2 tablespoons (2 × 15 ml spoon) finely chopped thyme

1 red, 1 yellow and 1 green pepper, all de-seeded and sliced

good olive oil, for frying

salt

butter with the garlic and herbs and then make a layer of them in the bottom of a deep serving dish, spooning over the garlicy butter.

Fry the sliced peppers in oil separately, one colour at a time, taking each out with a slotted spoon and putting to one side. Then, make a decorative lattice over the top of the tomatoes with half of the coloured peppers.

Dry the slices of aubergine and courgette with kitchen paper towelling and fry in olive oil until golden and soft. Place the aubergine and courgettes on top of the peppers in an overlapping spiral pattern. Finish by decorating the top with the rest of the peppers. Serve cool.

COURGETTE SOUFFLÉ CRÊPES

Basic recipe: 12 pancakes (see opposite), omitting the sorrel — Serves 6

Preparation time 40 minutes + 12–15 minutes baking

12 oz (350 g) courgettes, sliced thinly

1½ oz (40 g) butter

2 oz (50 g) plain flour

½ pint (300 ml) hot milk

3 eggs, separated

1 oz (25 g) parmesan cheese

12 pancakes

salt and pepper

Oven temperature:
Gas Mark 6/400°F/200°C

This dish is a real conversation stopper. If you want to convince your friends that vegetarian cookery can be gastronomic, just put this casually in front of them and count the converts.

Preheat the oven. Steam the courgette slices in a colander or steamer over simmering water for about 3 minutes so that they are cooked but still crisp. Melt the butter in a saucepan, stir in the flour and gradually add the hot milk, stirring all the time to get a smooth sauce. Season with salt and pepper and cook very gently for 5 minutes.

Take off the heat. Beat the egg yolks and stir into the mixture, then fold in the courgettes and half of the parmesan. Beat the egg whites until stiff and fold in.

Heap some of the mixture on to one half of each pancake and fold the other half over the top, then arrange in a buttered ovenproof dish. Bake for 12–15 minutes, until the soufflé mixture is puffy and browned. Sprinkle over the remaining parmesan and serve immediately.

BAKED EGGS IN COURGETTES

Preparation time 25–30 minutes | Serves 4

8 medium-size courgettes, cut into ¼-inch (5 mm) slices

2 oz (50 g) butter, melted

4 eggs

grated parmesan cheese

salt and pepper

Oven temperature:
Gas Mark 6/400°F/200°C

Although this dish has to be timed very precisely and served up immediately, it is well worth the trouble: the baked eggs have a softness which is an irresistable contrast to the crunchiness of the lightly-cooked courgettes. Serve with garlic bread.

Preheat the oven. Drop the slices of courgette into boiling water and parboil for 2 minutes. Drain. Line four 6-inch (15 cm) ramekin or individual ovenproof dishes with the slices, making a nest, and dribble the melted butter over them. Break an egg into the centre of each nest and season with salt and pepper. Sprinkle with a little parmesan and bake for 8–10 minutes or until the eggs are lightly set. Serve at once.

TANGY AVOCADO

Preparation time 10 minutes + chilling | Serves 4

2 ripe avocados

4 tablespoons (4 × 15 ml spoon) tomato ketchup

5–6 drops of Tabasco sauce, or to taste

juice of ½ lemon

To garnish:

chopped parsley

Although this is a disarmingly simple way to serve avocados, it is quite original. The tang of Tabasco is an excellent contrast to the bland avocado, in an easy hors d'oeuvre which is always popular.

Cut the avocados in half lengthways and remove the stones. Mix the ketchup with the Tabasco and lemon juice and pour into the cavities of the avocados. Sprinkle parsley over the sauce and serve chilled, on a bed of lettuce if you like.

Baked Eggs in Courgettes
Tangy Avocado

CAULIFLOWER WITH CORIANDER VINAIGRETTE

Preparation time 25 minutes + 1 hour marinating | Serves 4

For the dressing:

4 fl oz (110 ml) olive oil

1 tablespoon (15 ml spoon) white wine vinegar

2 teaspoons (2 × 5 ml spoon) coriander seeds, crushed

a small bunch of coriander leaves, chopped finely

salt and pepper

For the salad:

1 oz (25 g) creamed coconut

1 medium-size cauliflower, cut into florets

1 small head of fennel, sliced

4 large lettuce leaves, shredded

A fresh vegetable salad is always a delicious and light way to start a meal, and this is one of my favourites. It is unusual to use both the seed and the leaf of the coriander in the same dish, but personally I love the two together, different as they are. Serve this with warm Granary bread.

Stir the olive oil into the vinegar and season with salt and pepper. Add the crushed coriander seeds and chopped leaves and leave to marinate for at least an hour.

Pour 1 pint (600 ml) boiling water on to the coconut in a saucepan and stir until dissolved. Add the cauliflower florets and sliced fennel and simmer for about 4 minutes. Drain and cool.

Just before serving, dress the vegetables with the vinaigrette and serve on a bed of the shredded lettuce.

CREAMY OLIVE PÂTÉ

Preparation time 15 minutes + chilling | Serves 4

6 oz (175 g) canned cannellini beans

6 oz (175 g) cottage cheese

12 black olives, stoned

1 large clove of garlic, peeled

1 oz (25 g) sunflower margarine, melted

1 tablespoon (15 ml spoon) single cream

2 hard-boiled egg whites, chopped finely

freshly ground pepper

Pungent black olives and garlic give this dish a resonance of the Middle East. An excellent starter, it is served like a pâté, either with toast or with pitta bread.

Liquidise all the ingredients except the egg whites, which are just stirred into the purée. Chill before serving.

WHITE BEAN AND CHICK-PEA SALAD

Preparation time 20 minutes — Serves 4

For the purée:

2 × 14 oz (400 g) can of cannellini beans

2 large cloves of garlic, crushed

4 tablespoons (4 × 15 ml spoon) lemon juice

4 sprigs of chervil or parsley, chopped

salt and black pepper

For the salad:

14 oz (400 g) can of chick-peas

4 oz (100 g) white Cheshire cheese, cubed small

a small bunch of parsley, chopped

1 tablespoon (15 ml spoon) olive oil

1 tablespoon (15 ml spoon) lemon juice

8 lettuce leaves

This dip, served in a bowl in the middle of a plate of salad, is one of my most popular dinner party starters. It is different, it is tasty, it is appetising and invariably I am asked for the recipe: so here it is. Serve with warm pitta bread.

Blend or liquidise the cannellini beans with a little of the juice from the can, the garlic and the lemon juice. Season to taste with salt and pepper and sprinkle with the chopped chervil or parsley.

Drain the chick-peas and mix with the cheese, parsley, olive oil and lemon juice. Place the dip in a bowl in the centre of a plate and put the lettuce leaves around in a circle. Spoon the chick-pea mixture over the lettuce leaves and serve.

AVOCADO AND ROQUEFORT PUFFS

Preparation time 20 minutes + 15–20 minutes baking — Serves 4

1 large ripe avocado

4 oz (100 g) Roquefort cheese

7½ oz (175 g) packet of puff pastry, thawed if frozen

1 egg yolk, well beaten

Oven temperature:
Gas Mark 6/400°F/200°C

Crisp, golden triangles of puff pastry contain a delectably creamy filling; the strong taste of blue cheese contrasts with the smoothness of the avocado: a wonderful start to a party.

Preheat the oven. Mash the flesh of the avocado with the cheese. Roll out the pastry quite thinly and cut into 8 squares. Place one-eighth of the avocado mixture on each square and fold over to form a triangle (see diagram on page 46). Moisten the inside edges and seal by pressing down with a fork. Brush with the egg yolk and bake for 15–20 minutes until golden brown.

White Bean and Chick-pea Salad

Leeks en Croûte with Mushroom Purée

Avocado and Roquefort Puffs

Creamy Olive Pâté

LEEKS EN CROÛTE WITH MUSHROOM PURÉE

Preparation time 40 minutes — Serves 6

7½ oz (175 g) packet of puff pastry, thawed if frozen

6 medium-size leeks, washed and trimmed to the same length

1 egg yolk, beaten

For the purée:

1½ oz (40 g) butter

1 tablespoon (15 ml spoon) plain flour

¼ pint (150 ml) milk

8 oz (225 g) mushrooms, chopped roughly

5 fl oz (150 ml) carton of double cream

salt and pepper

Oven temperature:
Gas Mark 6/400°F/200°C

This is a stunning hors d'oeuvre and simple to make. A light pastry crust is wrapped around soft leeks, whose delicate flavour is perfectly in harmony with the creamy mushroom sauce. It would serve 3 as a main course.

Preheat the oven. Roll out the puff pastry quite thinly and cut into 6 oblongs the same length as the leeks. Wrap each leek up in a roll of pastry, leaving the ends open and sealing the joins with a little water. Place seam-side down on a well-greased baking tray, brush with the beaten egg yolk and bake for 15–20 minutes until puffed and golden.

Meanwhile melt ½ oz (15 g) of the butter in a heavy pan and gradually stir in the flour with a wooden spoon. Add the milk slowly, stirring until the sauce thickens. Season to taste and simmer over a very low heat for 5 minutes. Put to one side.

Sauté the chopped mushrooms in the remaining butter. Add the cream and simmer for 3–4 minutes so that it reduces a little. Season with the salt and pepper, then liquidise with the white sauce and heat up again in the pan. Pass around in a jug for spooning over the hot leek pastries.

GIANT STUFFED MUSHROOMS

Preparation time 35 minutes + 25 minutes baking — Serves 4

8 large mushrooms (or 4 huge ones)

1 oz (25 g) sunflower margarine

1 large onion, chopped

4 sticks of celery, chopped finely

2 teaspoons (2 × 5 ml spoon) mixed dried herbs

1 large clove of garlic, crushed

1 oz (25 g) dry-roasted peanuts, chopped

3 oz (75 g) cream cheese

1 egg yolk

grated parmesan cheese

salt and pepper

Oven temperature:
Gas Mark 4/350°F/180°C

Large mushrooms, heaped up with an aromatic filling, are a dramatic opening to a dinner party, and are best served piping hot. Since garlic is such a good team-mate of mushroom you can increase the quantity if you like, to make this even more delicious. Serve on squares of fried bread.

Remove the stalks from the mushrooms and chop them up finely. Heat the margarine in a pan and cook the onion gently, covered, for about 5 minutes until soft. Add the celery, mushroom stalks, herbs and garlic, and season with salt and pepper. Stir well and simmer, covered, for a further 10 minutes. Stir in the peanuts. Preheat the oven.

Cream the cheese and mix with the egg yolk. Stir in the celery mixture and fill the mushroom caps. Sprinkle with parmesan and bake for 25 minutes.

CORN COBS BAKED WITH HERB BUTTER

Preparation time 5 minutes + 45 minutes baking — Serves 4

4 corn cobs

4 oz (100 g) butter

4 tablespoons (4 × 15 ml spoon) mixed dried herbs

salt

Oven temperature:
Gas Mark 4/350°F/180°C

This is one of my very favourite simple recipes. For the amount of work put in, it offers excellent returns – a succulent, aromatic and delicious feast.

Preheat the oven. Spread each corn cob with butter and roll in the herbs to coat them well. Sprinkle with salt and wrap each one tightly in foil. Bake for 45 minutes, and don't forget the napkins (or even fingerbowls) when serving!

CHEESE AND LEEK SOUFFLÉ VOL-AU-VENTS

Pictured on page 4 — Serves 8

Preparation time 25 minutes + 10 minutes baking

2 leeks

32 small cooked vol-au-vent cases

1 oz (25 g) sunflower margarine

2 tablespoons (2 × 15 ml spoon) plain flour

¼ pint (150 ml) milk, warmed

a little cayenne pepper, to taste

a little grated nutmeg, to taste

2 oz (50 g) Gruyère cheese, grated

1 oz (25 g) parmesan cheese, grated

2 eggs, separated

salt and pepper

Oven temperature:
Gas Mark 6/400°F/200°C

These are sophisticated and make a party piece of great elegance. Chopped leek and a cheese soufflé mixture are encased in vol-au-vents to make a light and mouthwatering start to a meal.

Preheat the oven. Boil the leeks in a little water until cooked, about 5 minutes, then drain and chop finely. Put a little chopped leek in the bottom of each vol-au-vent case. Melt the margarine in a pan and stir in the flour. Gradually stir in the warmed milk until the sauce thickens. Bring to the boil and simmer very gently for 5 minutes, then season well with the cayenne, nutmeg, salt and pepper and add the grated cheeses.

Take the pan off the heat and stir in the egg yolks. Beat the whites until very stiff and fold into the mixture. Pile into the vol-au-vent cases and bake for 10 minutes or until risen and lightly set. Serve at once.

MILD LENTIL AND MIXED VEGETABLE CURRY

Basic recipe: Spiced Lentil Purée (page 57) Serves 4

Preparation time 35 minutes

1 oz (25 g) creamed coconut or 2 tablespoons (2 × 15 ml spoon) desiccated coconut

1½ lb (675 g) mixed vegetables of your choice, e.g. cauliflower, potatoes, courgettes, white cabbage, mushrooms, peas, carrots or broccoli, all chopped roughly

2 oz (50 g) sunflower margarine

2 onions, chopped

3 teaspoons (3 × 5 ml spoon) garam masala

1 pint (600 ml) Spiced Lentil Purée

This makes a beautiful meal, contrasting as it does the delicately spiced lentil purée with a coconut milk sauce. Use any vegetables in season. Serve with basmati rice and papadoms, and a fresh green salad to follow.

Pour ½ pint (300 ml) boiling water over the coconut and leave to dissolve.

Lightly cook all the chopped vegetables in boiling water, drain and put to one side.

Heat the margarine in a saucepan and cook the onions until soft. Stir in the garam masala, simmer for a minute and then gradually add the coconut milk. Add the vegetables and heat through. Add the lentil purée to the mixture, heat through again, stirring well, and serve.

AUBERGINE SOUFFLÉ

Preparation time 30 minutes + 45–60 minutes baking Serves 4

For the aubergine mixture:

2 large aubergines

2 teaspoons (2 × 5 ml spoon) salt

1 large clove of garlic, crushed

1 teaspoon (5 ml spoon) mixed dried herbs

2 tablespoons (2 × 15 ml spoon) double cream

1 oz (25 g) parmesan cheese, grated

4 large eggs, separated

For the white sauce:

½ oz (15 g) butter

1 tablespoon (15 ml spoon) plain flour

¼ pint (150 ml) milk, heated

salt and pepper

Oven temperatures:
Gas Mark 4/350°F/180°C
Gas Mark 7/425°F/220°C

This soufflé is one of the most successful I have ever offered up at a dinner party. It has a wonderful texture and taste, and is rich enough to need only a dish of little new potatoes and a salad to accompany it. A bottle of good red wine does not go amiss, either.

Preheat the oven to the lower setting and bake the aubergines, whole, for 30–40 minutes until quite soft. Meanwhile, make the white sauce: melt the butter in a heavy pan and gradually stir in the flour with a wooden spoon. Add the milk slowly, stirring until the sauce thickens. Season to taste and simmer over a very low heat for 5 minutes. Put to one side.

When the aubergines are cooked, cool and then scoop out the flesh. Turn the oven to the higher setting. Mix the aubergine flesh with the salt, garlic, herbs, cream and half of the grated parmesan. Stir this into the white sauce. Beat the egg whites until stiff. Beat the egg yolks thoroughly and stir them into the aubergine mixture, then fold in the stiffly beaten egg whites. Pour into a large, well-greased soufflé dish, sprinkle over the remaining parmesan and bake for 15–20 minutes. Serve immediately.

SESAME AUBERGINES WITH NOODLES

Preparation time 45 minutes + 15 minutes baking — Serves 6

For the base:

1 large or 2 medium-size aubergines

8 oz (225 g) noodles

1 lb (450 g) tomatoes, peeled and chopped

2 fl oz (50 ml) double cream

olive oil

salt and black pepper

For the topping:

1 oz (25 g) dried breadcrumbs

1 oz (25 g) sesame seeds

2 tablespoons (2 × 15 ml spoon) vegetable oil

a little sunflower margarine

salt

Oven temperature:
Gas Mark 6/400°F/200°C

Such an original combination of ingredients never fails to arouse comment, and in my experience it has never failed to win praise! The crunchy sesame topping contrasts with the soft aubergine and the delicately flavoured noodle base.

Slice the aubergines, sprinkle with salt and leave to sweat for 30 minutes. Meanwhile, boil the noodles until 'al dente' and drain. Liquidise the tomatoes with 1 teaspoon (5 ml spoon) salt, a little black pepper and the cream. Mix into the noodles and line the base of a casserole dish with the mixture. Preheat the oven.

Dry the aubergine slices thoroughly and fry in olive oil until soft and golden. Drain on kitchen paper towelling and place over the top of the noodles.

Mix the breadcrumbs and sesame seeds with salt to taste and the oil. Sprinkle over the top of the aubergines, dot with margarine and bake for 15 minutes.

JELLIED TOMATO RING

Preparation time 30 minutes + chilling — Serves 8

- *2 × 14 oz (397 g) can of tomatoes*
- *½ oz (15 g) gelatine*
- *5 fl oz (150 ml) carton of single cream*
- *½ pint (300 ml) mayonnaise*
- *juice of ½ lemon*
- *½ green pepper, chopped*
- *½ yellow pepper, chopped*
- *½ cucumber, peeled and diced*
- *3 celery sticks, sliced finely*
- *1 egg white, stiffly beaten*
- *salt and pepper*

This makes a wonderful buffet-supper party piece when filled with Lemon Rice Salad (page 83). Or, surround it with a salad of your choice and a basket of mixed breads, and a superb lunch is laid before you.

Purée the tomatoes with their juices in a blender or liquidiser. Put in a bowl. Dissolve the gelatine in 1 tablespoon (15 ml spoon) hot water and add to the tomatoes with the cream. Beat in the mayonnaise with a whisk and add a little lemon juice and seasoning to taste. Stir in the chopped vegetables and fold in the egg white. Pour into a 10-inch (25 cm) rinsed-out ring-mould and leave to set in the refrigerator for several hours. Turn out on to a platter before filling the centre, if you like, with Lemon Rice Salad.

Garlic Cheese Flan

Indonesian Rice Cakes

Jellied Tomato Ring

GARLIC CHEESE FLAN

Preparation time 40 minutes + chilling + 45 minutes baking Serves 4–6

For the pastry case:

4 oz (125 g) butter or vegetable margarine

6 oz (175 g) plain flour

4 tablespoons (6 × 15 ml spoon) cold water

salt

For the filling:

1 lb (450 g) fresh broccoli florets

1 oz (25 g) sunflower margarine

4 oz (100 g) mushrooms, sliced

a small bunch of parsley, chopped finely

1 large clove of garlic, chopped finely

4 oz (100 g) Cheddar cheese, grated

2 eggs

7 fl oz (210 ml) single cream

salt and pepper

Oven temperatures:
Gas Mark 4/350°F/180°C
Gas Mark 3/325°F/170°C

This is an up-market version of an ordinary quiche, made exceptional by the inclusion of broccoli and a little garlic.

Preheat the oven to the higher setting. To make the pastry, rub the fat into the flour and add a pinch of salt. Mix in the water and work to a smooth dough. (Alternatively, you can put all the ingredients in a blender and mix until the pastry has formed a ball.) Chill for 2 hours before rolling out and lining a 10-inch (25 cm) flan dish: lay the pastry over the dish with a rolling pin (1), press into the edges (2) and roll off the surplus pastry (3). Cover with foil, weight with beans and bake blind for 10 minutes. Take out to cool and turn the oven down to the lower setting.

Steam the broccoli florets in a colander or steamer over simmering water for about 5 minutes until cooked through but still crisp. (Or, boil for 5 minutes and drain.) Place them over the base of the pastry case. Heat the margarine in a frying pan and fry the sliced mushrooms quickly. Stir in the parsley and garlic and season with salt and pepper. Spread this mixture over the broccoli and cover with the grated cheese. Beat the eggs thoroughly and stir in the cream. Season with salt and pepper, pour over the top of the flan and bake for 45 minutes or until set. Serve warm or cold.

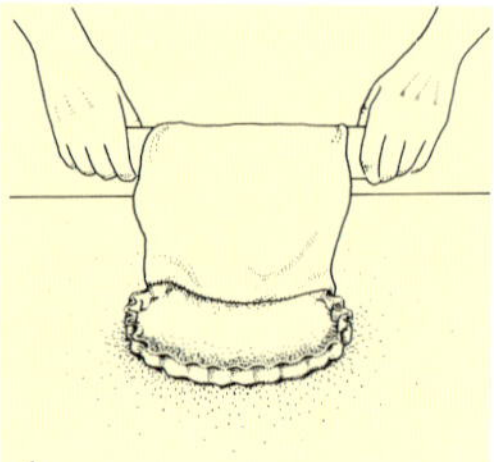

1

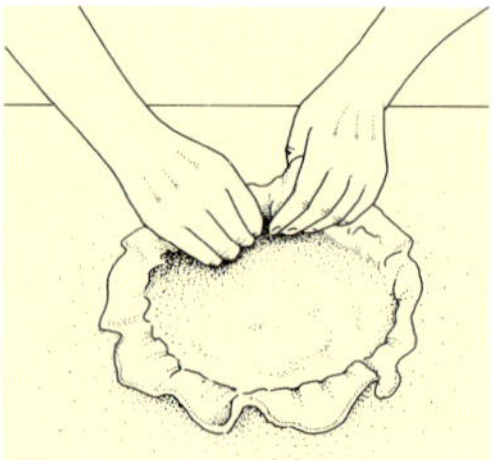

2

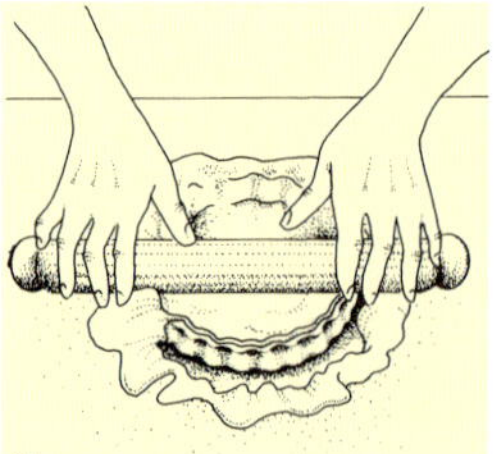

3

INDONESIAN RICE CAKES

Preparation time 45 minutes | Serves 4

1 pint (600 ml) water

2 oz (50 g) creamed coconut

12 oz (350 g) Patna or long grain rice

2 teaspoons (2 × 5 ml spoon) salt

1 teaspoon (5 ml spoon) mixed dried herbs

1 teaspoon (5 ml spoon) garam masala

½ cucumber, peeled and diced

1 small pepper, chopped

6 spring onions, chopped

To serve:

satay sauce

lettuce leaves, shredded

These rice cakes, unusual fare in the West, are typical of southern Indian and Malay food. They can be seasoned with all manner of spices, and you can experiment with different chopped vegetables of your choice. They have a lovely soft texture and can be served up with a variety of salads.

Boil the water and pour it over the creamed coconut in a pan. Stir until dissolved. Add the rice, salt, herbs and garam masala, cover and cook gently for 10–12 minutes. Add the chopped vegetables a few minutes before the end of the cooking time. When all the liquid is absorbed put the rice in a dish, cover with a plate, weight down and cool. Cut into 16 squares when cold. Spoon over the satay sauce, about 1 tablespoon (15 ml spoon) over each cake, and serve on a bed of shredded lettuce.

FOUR-CHEESE TAGLIATELLE

Preparation time 15 minutes | Serves 4

12 oz (350 g) tagliatelle

2 tablespoons (2 × 15 ml spoon) olive oil

3 oz (75 g) each of bel paese, mozzarella, dolcelatte and parmesan cheese, all diced

2 cloves of garlic, crushed

a small bunch of basil, chopped

salt and black pepper

I hardly dare to cook this because it is so delicious, so bad for the waistline, yet so enjoyable. So when you're in the mood to spoil yourself, your figure and your guests, throw calorie-caution to the winds and cook this dish. Don't forget the Chianti!

Boil the tagliatelle for 8 minutes or until 'al dente'. Drain. Heat the oil in a pan and toss the pasta in it. Add the cheeses and mix well over a gentle heat. Mix in the garlic and basil, and season to taste with salt and lots of black pepper. Carry on tossing for a minute or two to allow all the tastes to blend, and serve up on warm plates.

BLACK-EYED BEANFEAST

Serves 6

Preparation time 1 hour + 30 minutes cooking + soaking overnight

- *8 oz (225 g) black-eyed beans, soaked overnight*
- *6 tablespoons (6 × 15 ml spoon) vegetable oil*
- *1 teaspoon (5 ml spoon) cumin seeds*
- *½ teaspoon (2.5 ml spoon) cinnamon*
- *8 oz (225 g) onions, chopped*
- *4 cloves of garlic, sliced*
- *14 oz (397 g) can of tomatoes, chopped*
- *8 oz (225 g) mushrooms, sliced*
- *2 teaspoons (2 × 5 ml spoon) coriander seeds*
- *½ teaspoon (2.5 ml spoon) each of ground cumin, turmeric and cayenne pepper*
- *3 tablespoons (3 × 15 ml spoon) chopped fresh parsley*
- *salt and freshly ground pepper*

A feast indeed: this is one of the very best ways that I know of cooking beans, and it is just as good cold as hot. Serve it with Brussels Sprouts with Garlic and Parmesan (page 70) and Steamed Fennel with Light Ginger Sauce (page 72). Produce some fresh Granary bread and you have a meal fit for a king.

Drain the soaked beans in a pan with 2 pints (1.2 litres) fresh water. Bring to the boil and boil rapidly for 10 minutes.

Heat the oil in a saucepan and sizzle the cumin seeds and cinnamon in it for a few seconds. Add the onions and garlic and stir for a minute or two. Add the tomatoes, mushrooms and remaining spices and herbs. Season to taste. Simmer for 10 minutes. Add the beans with enough of their cooking liquid just to cover the mixture, and simmer gently for 30 minutes. Allow to stand for a while before serving.

Stuffed Courgettes with Red Pepper Sauce

Layered Vegetable Terrine

Black-eyed Beanfeast

LAYERED VEGETABLE TERRINE

Preparation time 45 minutes + 1½ hours baking — Serves 6

- *12 oz (350 g) fresh spinach, washed*
- *1 teaspoon (5 ml spoon) ground allspice*
- *6 eggs*
- *2 tablespoons (2 × 15 ml spoon) chopped chives*
- *1 lb (450 g) carrots, peeled and chopped*
- *1 lb (450 g) celeriac, peeled and chopped*
- *3 tablespoons (3 × 15 ml spoon) single cream*
- *salt and pepper*

For the green peppercorn sauce:

- *10 fl oz (284 ml) carton of double cream*
- *3 tablespoons (3 × 15 ml spoon) green peppercorns, crushed*
- *2 teaspoons (2 × 5 ml spoon) lemon juice*
- *salt*

Oven temperature:
Gas Mark 6/400°F/200°C

The pastel colours of this creation make it as much a work of art as something to eat! It is a lovely centre-piece to a dinner table, and is wonderful served with the creamy green peppercorn sauce.

Boil the spinach with a little water for 6–8 minutes and drain. Season the spinach with salt, pepper and ground allspice. Stir in 2 eggs, beaten, and the chopped chives.

Put the chopped carrots and celeriac in separate saucepans with boiling water to cover and cook until 'al dente'. Purée them lightly one at a time – the mixture should remain fairly coarse. Add half of the cream to each purée, then stir 2 eggs, beaten, into each one. Season both to taste. Preheat the oven.

Spread the carrot purée over the base of a well-greased 2½-pint (1.5-litre) loaf tin. Make another layer with the celeriac and finish with the spinach. Cook, standing in an ovenproof dish half-full of hot water, for 1½ hours. Allow to cool for at least 10 minutes before turning out.

To make the sauce, heat the cream gently in a pan, add the peppercorns and leave over a low heat for 5 minutes to infuse. Let cool, then add the lemon juice and salt to taste. Serve chilled, in a separate jug to pour over the warm or cold terrine.

STUFFED COURGETTES WITH RED PEPPER SAUCE

Preparation time 40 minutes — Serves 4

2 large or 4 medium-size courgettes

4 oz (100 g) cream cheese

2 oz (50 g) Gruyère cheese, grated

2 oz (50 g) chopped walnuts

3 eggs, separated

2 red peppers

salt and pepper

Oven temperature:
Gas Mark 6/400°F/200°C

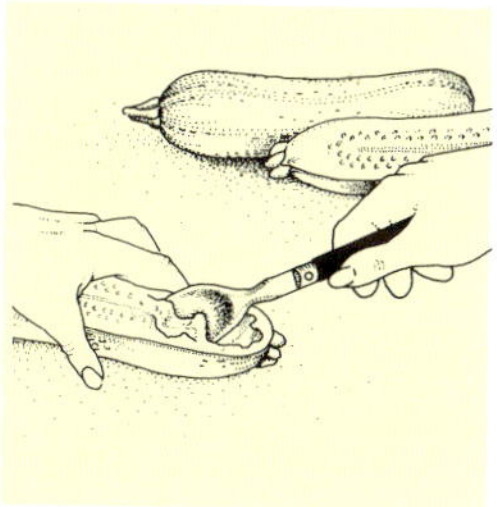

This cold party dish, prettily red and green, has subtle flavours. The red pepper sauce has a deliciously thick texture which is a marvellous foil to the courgettes with their cheesy, slightly crunchy filling. Serve it with Bright Bean Salad (page 80).

Preheat the oven. Cut the courgettes in half lengthways and scoop out the seeds to leave a boat-shape (see diagram). Sprinkle with salt and set to one side. Mash the cream cheese with the grated Gruyère and chopped walnuts and season with salt and pepper. Mix in the egg yolks thoroughly. Beat the egg whites until very stiff and fold into the cheese mixture.

Wipe the courgette halves dry and put one quarter of the cheese mixture into each hollow. Bake on a well-greased baking tray for 25–30 minutes, until set. Leave to cool.

While the courgettes are cooking, make the sauce. Boil the peppers, whole, for 10 minutes, then skin and de-seed them. Liquidise with 2 tablespoons (2 × 15 ml spoon) of the cooking water (adding a little more if required) to thin out. Add a pinch of salt to taste, cool and spoon over the cold courgettes.

SAFFRON RISOTTO

Preparation time 35 minutes — Serves 4

For the risotto:

½ teaspoon (2.5 ml spoon) saffron filaments

2 tablespoons (2 × 15 ml spoon) hot milk

2 tablespoons (2 × 15 ml spoon) vegetable oil

8 oz (225 g) basmati or risotto rice, well washed

3 oz (75 g) fried cashews

2 whole cardamom seeds, crushed

12 fl oz (350 ml) water

8 oz (225 g) peas

salt

For the egg rolls:

1 egg, beaten

2 tablespoons (2 × 15 ml spoon) milk

a little oil for greasing

salt and pepper

Saffron is the most precious spice in the world. Here, it gives a radiant gold colour to the rice with which it is cooked, and an unbeatable and distinctive taste. The risotto is garnished with decorative paper-thin egg rolls.

Soak the saffron in the hot milk. Heat the oil in a pan and stir the rice in it for a few minutes. Add the nuts and the crushed cardamom seeds, then pour in the water and add the peas with salt to taste. Mix once, then cover and cook slowly until the liquid is absorbed, about 20 minutes. Add the saffron in its milk and stir until well mixed and the rice grains cooked through.

Beat up the egg with a little milk and season with salt and pepper. In a large pan heat a tiny amount of oil, pour in the egg and make a paper-thin omelette with it (1). When it is cool, roll it up, cut it into thin strips (2) and decorate the risotto with these egg-whirls.

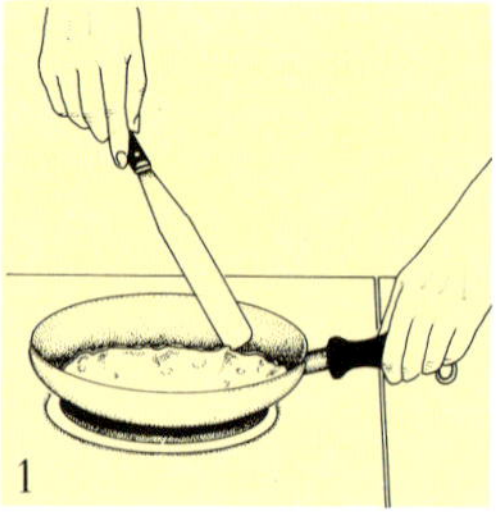

1

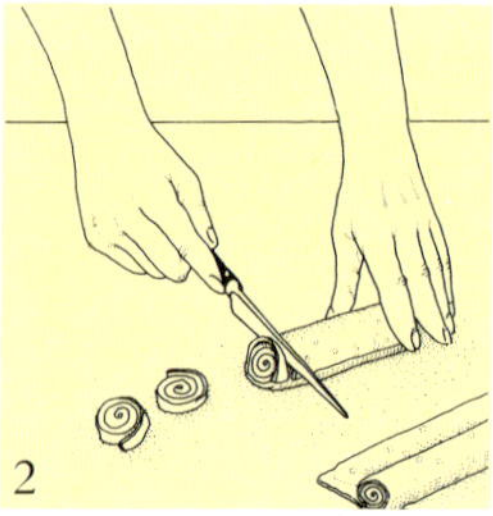

2

Saffron Risotto

ASPARAGUS PUFFS

Preparation time 20 minutes + 15–20 minutes baking   Serves 4

1 oz (25 g) sunflower margarine

2 tablespoons (2 × 15 ml spoon) plain flour

¼ pint (150 ml) milk

5 fl oz (150 ml) carton of double cream

1½ lb (675 g) fresh asparagus, cooked and chopped, or 2 × 12 oz (340 g) can of asparagus spears, chopped

12 oz (340 g) packet of puff pastry, thawed if frozen

1 egg, beaten

salt

Oven temperature:
Gas Mark 6/400°F/200°C

There is something about these crisp golden pastry puffs, filled with a tempting asparagus mixture, that delights all party guests whether or not they are vegetarian themselves. Serve with Stir-fried Cabbage with Mushrooms and Beansprouts (page 66), Spiced Okra (page 71) and a salad of your choice.

Make the sauce: melt the margarine in a pan, stir in the flour and add the milk gradually, stirring as the sauce thickens. Add the cream and simmer for 10 minutes, then season to taste with a little salt. Mix the chopped asparagus into the sauce and chill.

Preheat the oven. Roll the pastry out quite thinly and cut into 8 times 5-inch (12.5 cm) squares. Place one-eighth of the mixture on the centre of each square and fold over to make a triangle (see diagram). Moisten the inner edges with water and press down with a fork to seal. Brush with the beaten egg and bake on a well-greased baking tray for 15–20 minutes until they are golden brown.

TIROPITTA WITH SPRING ONION

Preparation time 25 minutes + 45 minutes baking — Serves 4

For the filling:

2½ oz (65 g) butter

3 tablespoons (3 × 15 ml spoon) plain flour

¾ pint (450 ml) milk, heated

8 oz (225 g) feta cheese

2 eggs, beaten

8 spring onions, chopped finely

salt and pepper

For the pastry:

8 sheets of Greek filo pastry

olive oil

Oven temperature:
Gas Mark 4/350°F/180°C

Greek cuisine gave us this version of cheese pie, with wafer-thin pastry topping a rich cheesy filling, and I have made it even more elegant with the addition of spring onions. The pie goes best, in my opinion, with a crisp lettuce and tomato salad and a glass of retsina or Sainsbury's Gerwürztraminer.

Preheat the oven. Melt the butter in a heavy saucepan and gradually stir in the flour with a wooden spoon. Add the milk slowly, stirring until the sauce thickens. Season to taste and simmer over a very low heat for 5 minutes. Take off the heat.

Mash the cheese and combine with the beaten eggs, white sauce and spring onions. Grease a 10-inch (25 cm) square baking tin and line it with 2 sheets of the pastry, brushing each one with oil. Pour in the filling and cover with the remaining sheets of pastry, oiled. Bake for 45 minutes and cut into squares to serve.

Alternatively, you can wrap individual portions of the cheese filling up in parcels of the oiled pastry sheets, folding in the ends to make them drip-proof, and brushing the tops with more oil before baking.

KEDGEREE WITH SUMMER VEGETABLES

Preparation time 35 minutes | Serves 6

3 tablespoons (3 × 15 ml spoon) vegetable oil

1 tablespoon (15 ml spoon) cumin seeds

4 cloves

4 cardamom seeds

4 black peppercorns

1-inch (2.5 cm) stick of cinnamon

1 teaspoon (5 ml spoon) turmeric

2-inch (5 cm) piece of root ginger, peeled and grated

2 large onions, chopped

4 oz (100 g) green lentils, soaked for a few hours and drained

4 oz (100 g) basmati rice, well washed

6 oz (175 g) each of 4 vegetables, e.g. cauliflower, peas, new potatoes, french beans, mange-tout peas, runner beans or courgettes

salt

The original Indian 'kitchri' is a soothing mixture of rice, lentils and spices, cooked until they are the consistency of mashed potato. In this recipe they are cooked for a shorter time so that they are still distinguishable but soft enough to make a delicious background to your favourite summer vegetables.

Heat the oil in a large saucepan and fry all the spices, except the turmeric and the ginger, until they splutter a little. Then add the turmeric, ginger and the onion and cook for a minute or two, stirring well. Add ¾ pint (450 ml) water and bring to the boil. Stir in the lentils, rice and all the chopped vegetables and simmer, covered, for 15–20 minutes or until the rice is cooked. Season to taste with salt and allow to stand for a while, covered, before serving. It is also excellent cold.

Kedgeree with Summer Vegetables
Okra and Courgettes in Lentil Sauce

OKRA AND COURGETTES IN LENTIL SAUCE

Basic recipe: Spiced Lentil Purée (page 57) Serves 4

Preparation time 20 minutes

1 lb (450 g) okra

1½ lb (675 g) courgettes, cut into ¼-inch (5 mm) slices

8 oz (225 g) french beans, cut into 1-inch (2.5 cm) lengths

1½ pints (900 ml) Spiced Lentil Purée

salt and pepper

This is almost the equivalent of a stew; a dish of lightly steamed vegetables coated in lentil purée. I have also made it with other combinations of vegetables, very successfully, but the combination of okra and courgettes is just right for a party dish. Serve with basmati rice and papadoms.

Steam the vegetables in a colander or steamer over simmering water until they are cooked through but still crisp, about 5 minutes. Heat the lentil purée and thin out with water as necessary, adjusting the seasoning to taste. Arrange the vegetables prettily in a dish and spoon the sauce over them.

PENNE WITH PEPPERS

Pictured on pages 4–5 Serves 4

Preparation time 30 minutes

1 red pepper

1 yellow pepper

2 cloves of garlic, sliced

6 tablespoons (6 × 15 ml spoon) olive oil

1 lb (450 g) penne (pasta quills)

4 tablespoons (4 × 15 ml spoon) grated parmesan cheese

a small bunch of coriander, chopped finely

salt and freshly ground black pepper

Personally I adore pasta, and I love to serve it as a speciality at a dinner party. This combination of peppers, garlic and coriander, with masses of black pepper, is strong and rustic.

Cut the peppers into quarters and grill them skin-side up until the skins blister and can be easily peeled off. Cut into little strips the same length as the penne.

Cook the garlic gently in 2 tablespoons (2 × 15 ml spoon) of the oil until soft, then stir in the peppers and cook for a minute or two. Season generously with salt and pepper, and add the rest of the oil.

Boil the penne until 'al dente' (10–15 minutes), drain and then toss in the pepper mixture. Stir in the grated cheese and the coriander, adjust the seasoning and serve at once.

RISOTTO WITH FENNEL AND PETITS POIS

Preparation time 40 minutes + a few hours soaking Serves 6

- *4 tablespoons (4 × 15 ml spoon) sunflower margarine*
- *1 onion, chopped finely*
- *a small bunch of coriander, chopped*
- *4 oz (100 g) lentils, soaked in cold water for a few hours*
- *4 oz (100 g) rice, washed*
- *2 heads of fennel, sliced*
- *8 oz (225 g) petits pois*
- *2 oz (50 g) Gruyère cheese, grated*
- *1–2 teaspoons (1–2 × 5 ml spoon) ground cumin*
- *salt*

A pale green dish of great elegance, which looks lovely on the table with glasses of chilled rosé wine. It is delicately flavoured with coriander and cumin, and the Gruyère has a delectable texture. Serve it with papadoms and a salad of your choice.

Heat the margarine in a saucepan and sauté the onion. Add the chopped coriander. Drain the lentils and stir in with the rice, then add the fennel and fry together for 5 minutes. Add 1 pint (600 ml) water and simmer for 10–15 minutes until the water is absorbed and the rice and lentils are cooked through but not mushy. Add the petits pois and cheese. Season with the ground cumin and salt to taste and stir well. Cook gently for a further 5 minutes and then keep warm until ready to serve.

NOODLES ORIENTAL STYLE

Preparation time 12 minutes Serves 4

- *6 oz (175 g) thin noodles*
- *4 medium-size courgettes, cut diagonally into slivers*
- *8 oz (225 g) okra*
- *8 oz (225 g) broccoli florets, sliced thinly*
- *2 tablespoons (2 × 15 ml spoon) sesame oil*
- *1 large clove of garlic, crushed*
- *½-inch (1 cm) piece of root ginger, peeled and grated*
- *2 tablespoons (2 × 15 ml spoon) soy sauce*

This, for all its simplicity, is a knockout. It is one of my personal favourites, partly because it is so satisfying to create such an original dish in such a short time! Serve it with a crisp green salad.

Cook the noodles as instructed on the packet. Drain and keep warm in a large serving dish. Steam the courgettes, okra and broccoli in a steamer or colander over a pan of simmering water until 'al dente'. Heat the oil in a saucepan and quickly stir all the vegetables in the oil until they are coated, adding the garlic, ginger and soy sauce. Pour this mixture over the hot, drained noodles, toss thoroughly and serve immediately.

SPINACH LAYERS

Preparation time 1¼ hours — **Serves 6**

For the spinach layer:

1½ lb (675 g) spinach, washed

3 tablespoons (3 × 15 ml spoon) double cream

3 tablespoons (3 × 15 ml spoon) grated parmesan cheese

3 large eggs, separated

For the mushroom layer:

2 oz (50 g) sunflower margarine

8 oz (225 g) mushrooms, sliced

2 tablespoons (2 × 15 ml spoon) double cream

salt and pepper

For the cottage cheese layer:

10 cashew nuts, ground

10 blanched almonds, ground

8 oz (225 g) cottage cheese

1 tablespoon (15 ml spoon) chopped parsley

1 tablespoon (15 ml spoon) chopped chives

salt to taste

Oven temperatures:
Gas Mark 4/350°F/180°C
Gas Mark 6/400°F/200°C

A certain degree of dedication is required to create this dish, as there is a lot of work involved. But, as always, it does pay off – the finished product proves the effort worthwhile. This dish has a fine variety of tastes and textures, and makes a delicious and substantial main course.

Boil the spinach in a little water and salt for 6–8 minutes and drain. Purée the cooked spinach in a blender or liquidiser and mix in the cream and 1 tablespoon (15 ml spoon) of the parmesan. Beat the egg yolks together and mix in well.

Heat the margarine in a pan and cook the mushrooms quickly for 1–2 minutes. Stir in the cream and season to taste.

Mix the ground nuts together well and stir into the cottage cheese with the herbs. Add salt to taste. Preheat the oven to the lower setting.

Put one-third of the spinach over the bottom of a large 8-inch (20 cm) greased soufflé dish, then make a layer with all the mushrooms, then another third of the spinach, then all the cottage cheese and finally the rest of the spinach. Bake for 10 minutes. Take out of the oven, turning this up to the higher setting.

Beat the egg whites until very stiff and fold in the remaining parmesan cheese. Pile on top of the layered mixture in the dish and cook for a further 10 minutes or until golden brown. Serve immediately.

Spinach Layers
Savoury Ratatouille Crumble

SAVOURY RATATOUILLE CRUMBLE

Preparation time 10 minutes + 20 minutes baking — Serves 2

1 large clove of garlic, crushed

13 oz (380 g) can of ratatouille

2 oz (50 g) sunflower margarine

4 oz (100 g) plain flour

1 heaped tablespoon (2 × 15 ml spoon) grated parmesan cheese

salt and pepper

Oven temperature:
Gas Mark 6/400°F/200°C

This is a dish for a special meal which can be made spontaneously because it is quick and easy to prepare, yet is as delicious as if you had spent hours of loving care over it. Serve it with Chicory and Fennel in Coriander Vinaigrette (page 87) and a bottle of good red wine.

Preheat the oven. Add the crushed garlic to the ratatouille and season with salt and pepper if required. Put in an ovenproof dish. Cream the margarine with the flour until crumbly, then stir in the parmesan. Season well with salt and pepper. Spread over the top of the ratatouille and press down evenly with the back of a fork. Bake for 20 minutes and serve.

CHEESE AND PIMENTO OMELETTE SOUFFLÉ

Preparation time 10 minutes — Serves 2

3 eggs, separated

2 oz (50 g) blue cheese, crumbled

2 canned pimentoes, chopped

2 tablespoons (2 × 15 ml spoon) double cream

1 oz (25 g) butter

salt and pepper

I reserve this recipe for those unexpected guests who deserve something more than just an ordinary omelette. It is deceptively quick to prepare, and goes well with Carrots with Garlic and Ginger (page 59) and Potatoes in Garlic and Parsley Butter (page 75). Or, just serve with a fresh green salad and a good bottle of red wine.

Beat the egg yolks with salt and pepper until creamy. Add the cheese, pimentoes and cream. Beat the egg whites until stiff and fold into the mixture.

Heat a large, heavy frying pan gently so that it is hot through, and melt the butter. Pour in the mixture and cook gently for a few minutes, running a spatula around the edge from time to time, being careful not to let the bottom burn. Place under a heated grill to set the top surface, then fold in half, cook for another minute or two over the heat and serve.

LEEK TIAN

Preparation time 15–20 minutes + 35–40 minutes baking Serves 4

1 lb (450 g) leeks, cut into ½-inch (1 cm) slices

4 oz (100 g) rice, washed and cooked

1 tablespoon (15 ml spoon) chopped parsley

4 oz (100 g) Cheddar cheese, grated

½ teaspoon (2.5 ml spoon) cayenne pepper (optional)

2 eggs

2–3 tablespoons (2–3 × 15 ml spoon) grated parmesan cheese

salt and pepper

To garnish:

chopped fresh herbs

Oven temperature:
Gas Mark 6/400°F/200°C

This delicious dish tastes rather like a textured baked custard. It can look sensational decorated with chopped herbs and surrounded with lightly steamed strips of coloured vegetables.

Preheat the oven. Cook the leeks in boiling water for 5–7 minutes until tender. Mix with the rice, add the parsley, Cheddar, cayenne (if used) and seasoning to taste. Beat the eggs thoroughly and mix them in. Put into a buttered heatproof dish and sprinkle with the parmesan. Bake standing in a dish half-full of hot water for 35–40 minutes. Rest for 5–10 minutes before turning out on to a platter. Garnish with the chopped herbs.

SIDE VEGETABLES

POTATOES ROMANOFF

Preparation time 15 minutes + 30 minutes baking — Serves 4

4 large potatoes
4 oz (100 g) cottage cheese
5 fl oz (150 ml) carton of soured cream
½ onion, chopped finely
1 teaspoon (5 ml spoon) sea salt
1 clove of garlic, crushed
a pinch of cayenne pepper
2 oz (50 g) Cheddar cheese, grated

To garnish:
chopped parsley

Oven temperature:
Gas Mark 4/350°F/180°C

This is a potato casserole, served hot, either to accompany a main course or as a lunch dish in its own right. It also makes a good salad – just combine the potatoes with the other, uncooked, ingredients and serve chilled.

Preheat the oven. Peel, boil and dice the potatoes. Mix all the ingredients together, place in an ovenproof dish and bake for 30 minutes. Garnish with the parsley and serve.

PETITS POIS WITH FENNEL

Preparation time 10 minutes — Serves 4

1 small head of fennel, sliced thinly
14 oz (400 g) frozen or canned petits pois
1½ oz (40 g) butter
1 clove of garlic, crushed
salt and pepper

This dish takes a matter of minutes to prepare, and is rich in terms of rewards – it is quite gastronomic.

Cut the slices of fennel into even-sized pieces about ½ inch (1 cm) long, and steam in a colander or steamer over a pan of simmering water for 5 minutes until they are cooked but still crunchy. Gently heat the petits pois with the liquid from the can, then drain and mix in the fennel. Melt the butter, add the garlic and season with salt and pepper. Pour over the petits pois and fennel, toss thoroughly and check the seasoning. Serve hot.

SPICED LENTIL PURÉE

Makes approx. 1½ pints (900 ml) — Serves 4

Preparation time 45 minutes + a few hours soaking

- *8 oz (225 g) red or green lentils, soaked for a few hours*
- *1 onion, sliced*
- *1 bay leaf*
- *1 whole fresh chilli*
- *1-inch (2.5 cm) piece of root ginger, peeled and bruised (beaten with a rolling pin)*
- *1 tablespoon (15 ml spoon) turmeric*
- *1–2 teaspoons (1–2 × 5 ml spoon) salt*
- *2 teaspoons (2 × 5 ml spoon) ground cumin*
- *2 teaspoons (2 × 5 ml spoon) ground coriander*

A very dear Indian girl-friend gave me this recipe: I have used it over and over again, and I love it every time. It goes beautifully with rice dishes and curries, and is delicious on its own with bread and a crisp green salad, for a light lunch.

Drain the soaked lentils and boil in a pan of water just to cover with the onion, bay leaf, chilli, ginger and turmeric. When they are soft, about 20 minutes, add the salt, cumin and coriander. Leave to stand, covered, for about 20 minutes, stirring occasionally until all the flavours have blended. The mixture will be quite runny like a purée, but should not be watery. Remove the chilli and bay leaf before serving.

CHINESE LEAVES WITH JUNIPER

Preparation time 10 minutes — Serves 4–6

- *1 chinese cabbage, sliced*
- *20 juniper berries, crushed*
- *2½ oz (65 g) butter, melted*
- *1 clove of garlic, crushed*
- *juice of ½ lemon*
- *a small bunch of parsley, chopped finely*
- *salt and pepper*

Juniper is our only native spice, and in my opinion it is much underused. It has a uniquely pungent flavour, which in this dish complements the delicacy of the chinese leaves and makes an exceptional side vegetable.

Simmer the cabbage with half of the juniper berries for 5 minutes or until cooked through. Meanwhile combine the rest of the juniper berries with the butter, garlic, lemon juice and parsley. Season to taste and toss the drained cabbage in the mixture.

TIMBALE OF MUSHROOMS

Preparation time 10 minutes + 45 minutes baking — Serves 4–6

- *2 oz (50 g) breadcrumbs*
- *1 oz (25 g) onion, chopped*
- *2 oz (50 g) butter*
- *4 oz (100 g) mushrooms, chopped finely*
- *2 oz (50 g) Cheddar cheese, grated*
- *1 clove of garlic, crushed*
- *4 eggs*
- *½ pint (300 ml) milk*
- *salt and pepper*

Oven temperature:
Gas Mark 4/350°F/180°C

A kind of mushroom mould, this looks very impressive turned out on to a platter and sliced like a cake into individual servings. The flavouring of mushroom with herbs, garlic and cheese is a classic one, but you could experiment using other vegetables and herbs.

Butter a soufflé dish or mould and sprinkle with 1 tablespoon (15 ml spoon) of the breadcrumbs.

Lightly cook the chopped onion in half of the butter in a saucepan. Add the remaining butter and sauté the mushrooms until their juice starts to run out. Add the cheese, garlic and the rest of the breadcrumbs. Season with salt and pepper and take off the heat.

Beat the eggs thoroughly and stir into the mushroom mixture. Heat the milk to boiling point and pour into the mixture in a thin stream, beating as you pour. Pour into the prepared mould and bake standing in a dish half-full of hot water for 45 minutes until a knife comes out clean. Let it rest for 5 minutes, then turn out on to a warm platter.

BABY BROAD BEANS WITH POPPY SEEDS

Preparation time 10 minutes — Serves 2

6 oz (175 g) baby broad beans

1 tablespoon (15 ml spoon) olive oil

1 tablespoon (15 ml spoon) poppy seeds

sea salt

We don't use poppy seeds adventurously enough with vegetables, in my opinion – they have a fine, delicate flavour and an appetising crunch, so try them with young broad beans in this dish, which can be served hot or cold.

Cook the broad beans in boiling water until 'al dente', about 5 minutes. Drain and toss in the oil. Sprinkle with the poppy seeds, add sea salt to taste and toss again before serving.

CARROTS WITH GARLIC AND GINGER

Preparation time 30 minutes — Serves 3–4

1 tablespoon (15 ml spoon) cumin seeds

1 lb (450 g) young carrots, sliced

1 large clove of garlic, crushed

1-inch (2.5 cm) piece of root ginger, peeled and grated

2 tablespoons (2 × 15 ml spoon) soy sauce

Oven temperature:
Gas Mark 5/375°F/190°C

This is my favourite way of preparing carrots – one of our best but most underrated vegetables. Use small, young carrots here, and see how the oriental flavouring transforms them!

Preheat the oven. Put the cumin seeds on a baking tray and cook for 5 minutes until lightly toasted, shaking them around from time to time. Put to one side.

Steam the carrots in a colander or steamer over simmering water until they are cooked but still crunchy. Mix the garlic and ginger into the soy sauce and toss the carrots in it, mixing well. Sprinkle with the cumin seeds just before serving.

SWEETCORN CHINESE STYLE

Preparation time 15 minutes | Serves 3–4

11 oz (330 g) can of sweetcorn

2 tablespoons (2 × 15 ml spoon) sesame oil

1 tablespoon (15 ml spoon) soy sauce

1 large clove of garlic, crushed

½-inch (1 cm) piece of root ginger, peeled and grated

8 spring onions, cut into ½-inch (1 cm) lengths

Quick and simple to make, this recipe transforms a can of sweetcorn into a dish of oriental flavour.

Drain the sweetcorn. Heat the oil in a saucepan and sauté the corn. When heated through, add the soy sauce, garlic and ginger and stir well. Add the spring onions and cook for 3–4 minutes, stirring well. Serve hot.

Baby Broad Beans with Poppy Seeds

Sweetcorn Chinese Style
Sweet Pepper Purée
Carrots with Garlic and Ginger

SWEET PEPPER PURÉE

Preparation time 20 minutes | Serves 3–4

3 large peppers, halved and de-seeded

4 large cloves of garlic, peeled

juice of ½ lemon

2 oz (50 g) sunflower margarine

salt and pepper

I love to serve this purée because it is so unusual, has the most beautiful aroma and is such a wonderful colour. Whether you use red or green peppers it is equally pretty – both have an intensely radiant colour.

Put the pepper halves in a pan with the whole cloves of garlic and cover with cold water. Bring to the boil, simmer for 10 minutes and then drain. Liquidise with the lemon juice and margarine, and season to taste. Serve hot or cold.

SPICY SPINACH PURÉE

Preparation time 15 minutes | Serves 4

1 lb (450 g) fresh spinach, washed

1 oz (25 g) sunflower margarine

½ teaspoon (2.5 ml spoon) ground cumin

½ teaspoon (2.5 ml spoon) ground coriander

½-inch (1 cm) piece of root ginger, peeled and grated

1 small clove of garlic, crushed

1 teaspoon (5 ml spoon) sea salt

Spinach becomes something very special when puréed with a delicate mixture of spices. This recipe is lovely with Garlic Cheese Flan (page 38).

Boil the spinach in a little water and salt for 6–8 minutes and drain. Melt the margarine in a pan and stir in the spices, ginger, garlic and salt. Purée with the cooked spinach, put back in the pan and heat through gently.

COURGETTES IN SPINACH SAUCE

Preparation time 25 minutes — Serves 4–6

1½ lb (675 g) small courgettes

1 lb (450 g) spinach, washed

5 fl oz (150 ml) carton of natural yogurt

1–2 cloves of garlic, crushed

½–1½-inch (1–4 cm) piece of root ginger, peeled and grated

salt

When courgettes are at their best in the summer try serving them in this lightly spiced spinach sauce. Serve hot or, even better, chilled.

Slice the courgettes thinly and boil them for just a few minutes so that they are still crisp and nutty in texture. Place in a serving dish. Boil the spinach in a little water and salt for 6–8 minutes. Drain and liquidise with the yogurt, garlic and ginger. Season to taste with salt and spoon over the courgettes.

CRUNCHY SLICED POTATOES

Preparation time 15 minutes — Serves 4

8 medium-size potatoes

1 tablespoon (15 ml spoon) garam masala

1 tablespoon (15 ml spoon) sea salt

oil for deep-frying

Hot, light little puffy crisps of spicy potato, these are worth cooking as a snack in their own right, as well as being a superb side vegetable for almost any main course.

Peel the potatoes and slice them thinly. Wipe them dry on kitchen paper towelling, sprinkle with garam masala and salt and deep-fry in very hot oil until puffed and golden. Drain on kitchen paper towelling and shake in a bowl with more salt and garam masala. Serve immediately.

ARTICHOKES DIJONNAISE

Preparation time 35–40 minutes | Serves 4

- *1½ lb (675 g) jerusalem artichokes, peeled*
- *1½ oz (40 g) sunflower margarine*
- *2 tablespoons (2 × 15 ml spoon) plain flour*
- *2 tablespoons (2 × 15 ml spoon) Dijon mustard*
- *¼ pint (150 ml) milk*
- *5 fl oz (150 ml) carton of single cream*
- *2 oz (50 g) Gruyère cheese, grated*

A combination of two delicate flavours – the unique nuttiness of jerusalem artichokes allies with fine Dijon mustard to make one of the best ways of serving this vegetable that I know.

Boil the artichokes until soft, about 15 minutes, slice and put to one side.

Melt the margarine in a saucepan and stir in the flour. Add the mustard and gradually stir in the milk, and then the cream, until the sauce thickens. Simmer gently for 5 minutes, then add the grated cheese and stir until it melts. Stir in the artichokes and heat through gently before serving.

Crunchy Sliced Potatoes

Artichokes Dijonnaise

Cabbage Masala

Courgettes in Spinach Sauce

CABBAGE MASALA

Preparation time 20 minutes — Serves 3–4

2 tablespoons (2 × 15 ml spoon) vegetable oil

8 oz (225 g) white cabbage, shredded very finely

1 onion, grated

2 teaspoons (2 × 5 ml spoon) garam masala

1 oz (25 g) pine nuts

sea salt

This third recipe in my trio of cabbage recipes reveals, I suppose, how fond I am of the vegetable – traditionally so misused, over-cooked and under-seasoned.

Heat the oil in a saucepan, add the cabbage and onion and toss over a medium heat until well-coated. Mix in the garam masala, turn down the heat, cover the pan and allow to steam for 10 minutes, stirring occasionally. Season to taste with salt and sprinkle with the pine nuts when ready to serve.

STIR-FRIED CABBAGE WITH MUSHROOMS AND BEANSPROUTS

Pictured on page 4 — Serves 4

Preparation time 20 minutes

3 tablespoons (3 × 15 ml spoon) sesame oil

1 small spring cabbage, shredded

2 tablespoons (2 × 15 ml spoon) soy sauce

8 oz (225 g) mushrooms, sliced

4 oz (100 g) beansprouts

Stir-frying is quick, light and clean, and seems to bring out the best in all vegetables. A touch of soy sauce is far better, in my opinion, than seasoning with salt.

Heat the oil in a pan and toss the shredded cabbage in it for a few minutes. Add the soy sauce and stir well. Cook for 3 more minutes, stirring, then add the sliced mushrooms and cook for a further 4 minutes. Stir in the beansprouts and cook for 1–2 minutes until they are heated through but still crisp. Add more soy sauce to taste if necessary, and serve immediately.

MALAY CABBAGE

Preparation time 20 minutes | Serves 4

1 small white cabbage, shredded

1 egg white

3 tablespoons (3 × 15 ml spoon) satay sauce

The typical Malay flavour of satay sauce, now available in bottles, goes well with slightly underdone cabbage. Both are slightly nutty in texture and are offset here by a soft background of egg white.

Steam the cabbage in a colander or steamer over simmering water so that it is cooked but still crisp and nutty. Put in a pan over a low heat. Stir in the egg white, mixing thoroughly until it begins to set. Stir in the satay sauce quickly, stir again and serve.

COURGETTES WITH MACE AND CREAM

Pictured on page 4 | Serves 3–4

Preparation time 20 minutes + 20 minutes baking

1 tablespoon (15 ml spoon) sesame seeds

4 large courgettes

1 teaspoon (5 ml spoon) mace

2 oz (50 g) butter

3 fl oz (75 ml) single cream

salt and pepper

Oven temperature:
Gas Mark 4/350°F/180°C

This is a dish of true elegance. Spicy mace is used to highlight a creamy sauce, which encloses slightly crisp slices of courgette.

Preheat the oven. Toast the sesame seeds on a baking tray for about 5 minutes until browned, shaking them around from time to time. Put to one side. Slice the courgettes thinly and put in an ovenproof dish. Sprinkle the mace over them, season with salt and pepper and dot with the butter. Bake, covered with foil, for 20 minutes. Heat the cream until warm, pour over the courgettes, heat through for a few more minutes on top of the oven and serve sprinkled with the toasted sesame seeds.

CREAMED CELERY WITH ALMONDS

Preparation time 20 minutes + 20 minutes baking | Serves 4

1½ oz (40 g) flaked almonds

1 small head of celery, sliced

1 can of condensed celery soup

2½ fl oz (60 ml) double cream

1 teaspoon (5 ml spoon) grated onion

1 whole canned pimento, chopped

a small bunch of parsley, chopped

Oven temperature:
Gas Mark 4/350°F/180°C

This method of cooking celery in a can of celery soup is quick and simple, yet full of flavour. The crunchy toasted almonds are a delightful finishing touch.

Preheat the oven. Toast the almonds on a baking tray for about 5 minutes until browned, shaking them around from time to time. Put to one side. Cook the celery in boiling water for 10 minutes and drain. Stir in all the rest of the ingredients except the almonds. Put in an ovenproof dish and bake for 20 minutes. Sprinkle the almonds over the top and serve.

Creamed Celery with Almonds

BRUSSELS SPROUTS WITH GARLIC AND PARMESAN

Preparation time 10 minutes + 20–25 minutes baking Serves 3–4

1 lb (450 g) brussels sprouts

1½ oz (40 g) butter

3 tablespoons (3 × 15 ml spoon) grated parmesan cheese

2 large cloves of garlic, crushed

Oven temperature:
Gas Mark 4/350°F/180°C

The simple touch of garlic and cheese transforms the mundane sprout into an elegant vegetable with a distinctly continental taste.

Preheat the oven. Parboil the sprouts in a pan of boiling water for 3 minutes and drain. Put in an ovenproof dish with the butter, parmesan and garlic, and toss well. Cover the dish and bake for 20–25 minutes.

CHUNKY SPICED CORN COBS

Preparation time 40 minutes Serves 4

4 tablespoons (4 × 15 ml spoon) vegetable oil

4 corn cobs, cut into 2-inch (5 cm) lengths

1 large onion, chopped

a small bunch of fresh coriander, chopped

2 cloves of garlic, crushed

1-inch (2.5 cm) piece of root ginger, peeled and grated

5 fl oz (150 ml) carton of natural yogurt

A highly original way of dealing with corn on the cob – it is extremely more-ish and I invariably end up eating far more of it than I rightly should!

Heat the oil in a pan and fry the pieces of corn cob for about 10 minutes, turning often. Remove from the pan. Add the onion and fry until soft, then add the coriander, garlic and ginger. Stir well. Add the yogurt and when well mixed in replace the corn cobs and poach them gently in the sauce for 20 minutes.

LEMON RICE WITH SPINACH

Preparation time 30 minutes | Serves 4

8 oz (225 g) basmati rice

1 lb (450 g) fresh spinach, washed

juice of 1 lemon

2 tablespoons (2 × 15 ml spoon) vegetable oil

2-inch (5 cm) piece of root ginger, peeled and grated

1 fresh chilli, chopped

2 teaspoons (2 × 5 ml spoon) turmeric

2 teaspoons (2 × 5 ml spoon) ground coriander

1 teaspoon (5 ml spoon) mustard seeds

1 teaspoon (5 ml spoon) coriander seeds

salt

The flavour of lemon goes exceptionally well with rice, and the sizzling spices that top this delectable mixture give it an extra bite.

Boil the rice until cooked, about 10–15 minutes. Boil the spinach with a little water and salt for 6–8 minutes and drain. Purée in a blender and mix with the cooked rice. Stir in the lemon juice and salt to taste. Heat the oil in a frying pan, add the ginger, chilli and spices and sizzle until they split and crackle a little. Pour over the top of the rice and spinach and serve at once.

SPICED OKRA

Preparation time 20 minutes | Serves 4

2 oz (50 g) creamed coconut

1 pint (600 ml) boiling water

8 oz (225 g) okra

2 tablespoons (2 × 15 ml spoon) vegetable oil

2 small dried chillies

1 clove of garlic, crushed

1 teaspoon (5 ml spoon) each of cumin seeds, mustard seeds and poppy seeds

Okra is a delicate, interesting vegetable and always a treat, I think, served up with a special dinner. Here, the cooking in coconut cream adds to their softness, and the heat of the spices lifts their blandness. It's worth trying this recipe with other vegetables too, such as french beans, cauliflower or white cabbage.

Dissolve the creamed coconut in the boiling water in a pan, add the okra and simmer until tender, about 6–8 minutes. Drain. Heat the oil in a frying pan and brown the chillies, garlic and seeds in it until they spit and begin to turn golden. Remove the whole chillies, pour over the cooked okra and toss well. Serve hot or cold.

BEETROOT WITH ORANGE SAUCE

Preparation time 30 minutes | Serves 4

1 lb (450 g) ready-cooked beetroot (not in vinegar), cut into strips

For the orange sauce:

8 oz (225 g) dark brown sugar

¼ pint (150 ml) malt vinegar

1 tablespoon (15 ml spoon) cornflour

juice and grated rind of 3 oranges

Oven temperature:
Gas Mark 2/300°F/150°C

Thin strips of beetroot coated with fresh orange sauce are two complementary tastes: the one earthy, the other light and tangy. It is even better the next day.

Put the strips of beetroot in an ovenproof dish. Preheat the oven.

Mix the sugar with the vinegar in a saucepan over a gentle heat and simmer for 5 minutes. Mix the cornflour with a little orange juice and add the rest of the juice to the pan with the grated rind. Simmer for a further 5 minutes, then stir in the cornflour mixture and cook, stirring, until the mixture has thickened. Pour over the beetroot and warm through in the oven for about 5–10 minutes, or until ready to serve.

STEAMED FENNEL WITH LIGHT GINGER SAUCE

Preparation time 20 minutes | Serves 3–4

1 head of fennel, sliced

For the sauce:

2 tablespoons (2 × 15 ml spoon) sesame oil

4 spring onions, cut into ¼-inch (5 mm) slices

½-inch (1 cm) piece of root ginger, grated

1 clove of garlic, crushed

1 tablespoon (15 ml spoon) soy sauce

Fennel is, to my mind, a divine vegetable with the most beautiful flavour, especially when it is cooked. This dish is wonderful served warm or cold.

Steam the fennel in a colander or steamer over simmering water for 5–8 minutes until lightly cooked through. Heat the oil in a frying pan and sauté the sliced spring onions, then stir in all the other ingredients. Pour over the fennel and toss well.

Beetroot with Orange Sauce
Baked Onion with Cumin Seeds
Steamed Fennel with Light Ginger Sauce

BAKED ONION WITH CUMIN SEEDS

Preparation time 5 minutes + 45 minutes baking — Serves 4

8 medium-size onions

4 tablespoons (4 × 15 ml spoon) red wine

approx. 6 tablespoons (6 × 15 ml spoon) water

1 teaspoon (5 ml spoon) salt

2 tablespoons (2 × 15 ml spoon) cumin seeds

Oven temperature:
Gas Mark 6/400°F/200°C

The sweetness of baked onion makes a marvellous marriage with cumin seed; the kitchen is filled during cooking with the sweet aromas of both. This dish is also very good cold, as an addition to a buffet table.

Preheat the oven. Put the whole, unpeeled onions in a pan of water, bring to the boil and simmer for 2 minutes. Drain and skin them. Put in an ovenproof dish with the wine, water, salt and cumin seeds and bake for 45 minutes or until soft, turning from time to time and adding more water if it begins to dry out. Serve hot.

DEEP-FRIED CAULIFLOWER MASALA

Preparation time 30 minutes + standing — Serves 4

2 oz (50 g) plain flour

½ teaspoon (2.5 ml spoon) salt

1 tablespoon (15 ml spoon) garam masala

1½ tablespoons (1–2 × 15 ml spoon) vegetable oil

3 fl oz (75 ml) water

1 medium-size cauliflower, cut into florets

1 egg white

oil for deep-frying

A light, spicy batter encases soft florets of cauliflower in a mouth-watering combination.

To make the batter: sift the flour into a bowl with the salt and garam masala. Stir in the oil and gradually add the water, stirring until the mixture is thick and creamy. Stand in a cool place for 2 hours, then add a little extra water, about 1–2 tablespoons (1–2 × 15 ml spoon) to thin out.

Cook the cauliflower florets in boiling water until 'al dente'. Drain and dry. Beat the egg white until it is very stiff and fold into the batter. Dip the florets in the batter so that they are well coated, and deep-fry in hot oil until golden brown and crisp. Drain on kitchen paper towelling and serve immediately.

POTATOES IN GARLIC AND PARSLEY BUTTER

Preparation time 30 minutes | Serves 3–4

1 lb (450 g) new potatoes

3 oz (75 g) butter

2 cloves of garlic, crushed

a bunch of parsley, chopped

1 tablespoon (15 ml spoon) grated parmesan cheese

sea salt and pepper

Oven temperature:
Gas Mark 4/350°F/180°C

The classic garlic and parsley butter traditionally served on snails is wonderful and should be put to other uses. Used here, it makes one of the best potato dishes that I know, especially if you can find young, waxy new potatoes.

Preheat the oven. Boil the potatoes lightly so that they are cooked but still crunchy, and slice them. Melt the butter in a frying pan and stir in the garlic and parsley. Cook gently for a few minutes and then season to taste with sea salt and pepper. Pour over the potatoes, sprinkle with the parmesan and bake for 5–10 minutes.

POTATOES GRUYÈRE

Preparation time 15 minutes + 1½ hours baking | Serves 4

6 large new potatoes

½ pint (300 ml) soured cream

5 oz (150 g) Gruyère cheese, grated

1 small onion, chopped finely

2 tablespoons (2 × 15 ml spoon) chopped chives

2 tablespoons (2 × 15 ml spoon) dried breadcrumbs

salt and pepper

To garnish:

a sprig of parsley

Oven temperature:
Gas Mark 3/325°F/170°C

Slowly cooked in soured cream with Gruyère, the full flavour of new potatoes is developed to its finest in this dish, which is rich, warming and sustaining.

Preheat the oven. Slice the potatoes thinly. Mix together the cream, cheese, onion and chives and season to taste. In an ovenproof dish, make layers of the potatoes and the cheese mixture, ending with the cheese on top. Sprinkle with the breadcrumbs, cover and bake for 1½ hours. Garnish with parsley and serve.

HERBED CUCUMBERS

Preparation time 15 minutes — Serves 4

2 tablespoons (2 × 15 ml spoon) vegetable oil

1 cucumber, peeled and diced

1 small onion, sliced thinly

2 tablespoons (2 × 15 ml spoon) chopped fresh herbs

½ teaspoon (2.5 ml spoon) Tabasco sauce

1 teaspoon (5 ml spoon) salt

I love cooked cucumber, it acquires a unique texture and glistens transparently on the plate. The taste of cucumber is quite different after cooking, and is delicious with freshly picked summer herbs.

Heat the oil in a pan and toss the cucumber and onion in it for 3 minutes, stirring all the time. Sprinkle in the herbs, Tabasco and salt. Cover and steam over a low heat for 4 minutes, shaking the pan from time to time. Serve immediately.

CUMIN CAULIFLOWER

Preparation time 15 minutes — Serves 4

1 medium-size cauliflower, cut into florets

1 tablespoon (15 ml spoon) sesame oil

1 teaspoon (5 ml spoon) turmeric

2 teaspoons (2 × 5 ml spoon) cumin seeds

Crisp and spicy, with the added sweetness of cumin, this way of preparing cauliflower is refreshingly different, yet quick and easy to prepare.

Cook the cauliflower florets in boiling water until 'al dente' and drain. Heat the oil with the turmeric in a frying pan, add the cumin and cook until crisp. Pour over the florets of cauliflower and stir so that they are well-coated. Serve immediately.

Potatoes Gruyère
Herbed Cucumbers
Cumin Cauliflower

COLD CHOUCROUTE

Basic recipe: egg rolls (page 44) — Serves 6

Preparation time 35 minutes + chilling

1 spanish onion, chopped finely

2 tablespoons (2 × 15 ml spoon) vegetable oil

1 lb (450 g) canned sauerkraut, drained

½ pint (300 ml) vegetable stock

1 clove of garlic, chopped

3 tablespoons (3 × 15 ml spoon) olive oil

2 tablespoons (2 × 15 ml spoon) cider vinegar

To garnish: *egg rolls*

An unusual salad, this one, and refreshingly sharp in flavour, which is why the soft egg roll garnish goes so well with it. A marvellous summer buffet dish.

Sauté the onion in the oil in a saucepan until softened and stir in the sauerkraut, stock and garlic. Simmer for 20 minutes and cool. Add the oil and the vinegar and toss well. Serve chilled, garnished with the egg rolls.

MIXED VEGETABLE SALAD WITH PEANUT SAUCE

Preparation time 20 minutes — Serves 4

½ oz (15 g) creamed coconut

½ pint (300 ml) boiling water

4 oz (100 g) salted peanuts

½ teaspoon (2.5 ml spoon) salt

a little single cream

1½ lb (675 g) mixed vegetables, e.g. white cabbage, french beans, spinach leaves, beansprouts, courgettes, spring onions, peas or broad beans, all sliced or shredded

This is a salad with a difference, one that can be made at any time of the year with whatever vegetables are in season. In the winter, the addition of paper-thin slices of raw root vegetables is lovely – try jerusalem artichokes, baby turnips, potatoes and onions.

Dissolve the creamed coconut in the boiling water. Liquidise the nuts, salt and coconut 'milk' together until you have a smooth paste. Boil in a pan for 2 minutes and thin out as required with single cream. Pour over the sliced and shredded vegetables and toss thoroughly.

COLD STUFFED TOMATOES

Preparation time 15 minutes + chilling — Serves 4

- *8 medium-size tomatoes*
- *1 tablespoon (15 ml spoon) tahina paste*
- *2 oz (50 g) natural yogurt*
- *1 teaspoon (5 ml spoon) cider vinegar*
- *2 oz (50 g) curd cheese*
- *a small bunch of coriander, chopped finely*
- *1 clove of garlic, chopped*
- *1 tablespoon (15 ml spoon) soy sauce*
- *4 oz (100 g) button mushrooms, diced small*

Good as a side salad or for a picnic, these nourishing delicacies are full of tastiness, and beguilingly easy to prepare. Serve on a bed of shredded lettuce.

Cut a slice off the tops of the tomatoes and scoop out the flesh and the seeds. Sprinkle with salt and leave upside-down to drain for 10 minutes. Mix the tahina with the yogurt and vinegar and mash into the curd cheese. Mix in the coriander, garlic and soy sauce and finally stir in the diced mushrooms. Pack into the rinsed, hollowed-out tomatoes and chill.

MUSHROOMS STUFFED WITH AUBERGINE PURÉE

Preparation time 15 minutes + 1 hour baking + cooling — Serves 4

- *2 large aubergines*
- *2 cloves of garlic, peeled*
- *2 tablespoons (2 × 15 ml spoon) olive oil*
- *3 tablespoons (3 × 15 ml spoon) natural yogurt*
- *juice of 1 lemon*
- *2 tablespoons (2 × 15 ml spoon) chopped parsley*
- *8 large flat mushrooms, with the stalks removed*
- *salt and pepper*

Oven temperatures:
Gas Mark 3/325°F/170°C
Gas Mark 6/400°F/200°C

This is an unusual salad to serve as a side plate or as part of a buffet table. It has a lovely soft, creamy texture and a delicate taste. It is also good served hot.

Preheat the oven to the lower setting. Bake the aubergines, whole, for 35–45 minutes until soft. Cool, cut in half and scoop out the pulp. Liquidise this with the garlic, oil, yogurt and lemon juice. Add the parsley and season to taste. Turn the oven to the higher setting.

Sprinkle the mushrooms with salt and pepper, cover with foil and bake for 10 minutes. Cool and then fill with the aubergine mixture.

BRIGHT BEAN SALAD

Preparation time 30 minutes Serves 4

2 oz (50 g) rice

4 oz (100 g) french beans

2 oz (50 g) each of canned red kidney beans, aduki beans and black-eyed beans, all drained

4 oz (100 g) sweetcorn

16 black olives, stoned and halved

a bunch of mixed fresh herbs, chopped finely

8 crisp lettuce leaves (optional)

For the dressing:

5 fl oz (150 ml) carton of natural yogurt

1 teaspoon (5 ml spoon) ground cumin

1 teaspoon (5 ml spoon) ground coriander

There are so many variations of bean salad, with so many richly coloured pulses to choose from, that you can improvise eternally. However, here is just one selection from the many.

Boil the rice for about 10–15 minutes and drain. Steam the french beans in a colander or steamer over simmering water until 'al dente', about 5 minutes. Cut into 1-inch (2.5 cm) lengths. Mix the rice, canned beans, sweetcorn, french beans and olives together and add the herbs. Arrange on a dish, surrounded by lettuce leaves if you like. Mix the dressing ingredients together and pour over the salad.

Bright Bean Salad

SPICED LENTIL AND PINEAPPLE SALAD

Basic recipe: Spiced Lentil Purée (page 57) — Serves 4

Preparation time 15 minutes + chilling

7 oz (200 g) can of pineapple

8 large lettuce leaves

¾ pint (450 ml) Spiced Lentil Purée

Being such a devotee of the Spiced Lentil Purée I have experimented with many ways of eating it cold as well as hot. This is one of the most exciting combinations, and has the virtue of possessing a soft, moist texture that contrasts well with other more crunchy salads.

Drain and chop the pineapple. Shred the lettuce leaves and blanch them in boiling water for a minute. Mix with the lentil purée, add the pineapple and serve chilled.

TOMATO AND GHERKIN SALAD WITH YOGURT

Preparation time 20 minutes + chilling — Serves 2

3 teaspoons (3 × 5 ml spoon) cumin seeds

3 large tomatoes

3 large gherkins, cut into fine strips, ½ inch (1 cm) long

½ onion, chopped finely

5 fl oz (150 ml) carton of natural yogurt

1 tablespoon (15 ml spoon) finely chopped parsley

Oven temperature:
Gas Mark 5/375°F/190°C

This salad goes well with a rich main course and is a welcome addition to a buffet of mixed salads, especially in the summer since it is so refreshing!

Preheat the oven. Lightly toast the seeds on a baking tray for about 5 minutes, shaking them around from time to time. Pour boiling water over the tomatoes in a bowl, stand for a few seconds and then drain, skin and chop them. Mix all the ingredients together and serve chilled.

LEMON RICE SALAD

Preparation time 20 minutes + chilling Serves 4

8 oz (225 g) basmati rice, well washed

1 bay leaf

1 teaspoon (5 ml spoon) turmeric

1-inch (2.5 cm) piece of root ginger, peeled and grated

juice of ½ lemon

2 oz (50 g) pine nuts

6 spring onions, chopped

A golden salad with the lovely flavour of basmati rice and the added crunch of pine nuts. The lemon juice bleaches the turmeric so that the resulting colour is like saffron.

Boil the rice with the bay leaf, turmeric and ginger for 8–10 minutes. Cool a little when it is done, then add the lemon juice, pine nuts and spring onions. Chill.

BEETROOT WITH YOGURT AND HAZELNUTS

Preparation time 15 minutes + chilling Serves 4

3 oz (75 g) hazelnuts

8 oz (225 g) ready-cooked beetroot (not in vinegar), cut into julienne strips

a small bunch of mixed fresh herbs, chopped finely

5 fl oz (150 ml) carton of natural yogurt

1 teaspoon (5 ml spoon) horseradish sauce

sea salt and black pepper

Oven temperature:
Gas Mark 5/375°F/190°C

The juice from the beetroot turns the yogurt a beautiful pink colour, which is offset by the fresh green of the herbs. The combination of beetroot and hazelnuts makes a rich and autumnal salad.

Preheat the oven. Toast the hazelnuts on a baking tray for about 5 minutes, shaking them around from time to time. Chop finely. Mix all the ingredients together and season to taste. Serve chilled.

SHREDDED LEEK SALAD

Preparation time 15 minutes + marinating | Serves 6

1 lb (450 g) leeks, washed and trimmed

1 teaspoon (5 ml spoon) French mustard

1 tablespoon (15 ml spoon) white wine vinegar

4 fl oz (110 ml) olive oil

2 tablespoons (2 × 15 ml spoon) double cream

sea salt and freshly ground black pepper

I am very fond of raw vegetables, but only recently experimented with raw leeks. When shredded very finely they are quite delicious.

Cut the leeks into 2-inch (5 cm) lengths and then slice them very thinly downwards, starting in the centre and working outwards so that you have long thin strands of leek.

Mix the mustard, vinegar and oil together well. Add the cream and season liberally with sea salt and freshly ground black pepper. Toss the leeks in the dressing and leave in the refrigerator to marinate for a few hours.

Tomato and Gherkin Salad with Yogurt

Beetroot with Yogurt and Hazelnuts

Lemon Rice Salad

Shredded Leek Salad

ARTICHOKES À LA GRECQUE

Preparation time 25 minutes + chilling — Serves 4

- *¾ pint (450 ml) water*
- *4 tablespoons (4 × 15 ml spoon) olive oil*
- *4 tablespoons (4 × 15 ml spoon) lemon juice*
- *½ teaspoon (2.5 ml spoon) salt*
- *a bouquet of herbs and spices tied in a muslin bag, e.g. parsley, celery leaves, fennel, thyme, 12 peppercorns and 6 coriander leaves*
- *1 lb (450 g) jerusalem artichokes, peeled and sliced into julienne strips*

'À la grecque', with its characteristic flavour of coriander seeds, is a classic way of cooking all sorts of vegetables. I think that it lends itself particularly well to the earthy flavour of jerusalem artichoke.

Simmer the water, oil, lemon juice, salt and bag of herbs and spices in a saucepan for 10 minutes. Add the artichokes and cook for 6–8 minutes until tender but still crisp. Remove the artichokes and bag with a slotted spoon and boil the liquid hard to reduce it. Pour over the artichokes and leave to cool. Serve chilled.

COURGETTE AND LEEK SALAD WITH BLUE CHEESE DRESSING

Preparation time 15 minutes + cooling — Serves 4

- *12 oz (350 g) small courgettes, sliced*
- *4 medium-size leeks, trimmed and cut into ½-inch (1 cm) slices*

For the blue cheese dressing:

- *2 oz (50 g) Danish blue cheese*
- *1 teaspoon (5 ml spoon) French mustard*
- *1 tablespoon (15 ml spoon) cider vinegar*
- *2 fl oz (50 ml) olive oil*

The best time of the year to make this salad is in early autumn, on those pale but bright days when the leaves are golden and the evenings are drawing in – when late courgettes are still around, and the first of the leeks are to be found.

Steam the vegetables in a colander or steamer over simmering water for 4–5 minutes until tender but still nutty. Leave to cool.

Mash the cheese and mustard with the vinegar until it is like a purée. Gradually stir in the oil until the mixture is quite smooth. Dress the vegetables when cool.

CHICORY AND FENNEL IN CORIANDER VINAIGRETTE

Preparation time 15 minutes + standing Serves 4

2 sticks of chicory, sliced

1 head of fennel, sliced finely

1 Webbs lettuce heart, shredded

a small bunch of fresh coriander, chopped finely

For the coriander vinaigrette:

4 fl oz (110 ml) olive oil

3 teaspoons (3 × 5 ml spoon) white wine vinegar

2 teaspoons (2 × 5 ml spoon) coriander seeds, crushed

salt and pepper

This is a fine salad for elegant summer meals, combining three distinctive yet subtle tastes.

Mix all the salad ingredients together. Stir the oil slowly into the vinegar, adding salt and pepper to taste, so that the mixture is well-blended. Stir in the crushed coriander seeds, adjust the seasoning and leave to stand before dressing the salad.

MEAUX POTATO SALAD

Preparation time 20 minutes + chilling Serves 4

1½ lb (675 g) small new potatoes, washed

8 oz (225 g) cottage cheese, mashed

5 fl oz (150 ml) carton of natural yogurt

6 tablespoons (6 × 15 ml spoon) moutarde de Meaux

Moutarde de Meaux is famous for its gastronomic quality, and added to creamy cottage cheese it makes a mouth-watering dressing for waxy new potatoes.

Boil the potatoes, then drain, cool and slice them. Mix the mashed cottage cheese with the yogurt, stir in the mustard and spoon over the potatoes. Mix well and chill.

CASHEW NUT SALAD WITH ORANGE DRESSING

Preparation time 20 minutes Serves 4

For the salad:

4 oz (100 g) cashew nuts

4 large tomatoes, peeled and sliced

1 small head of fennel, sliced finely

1 lettuce heart, chopped

a small bunch of watercress, trimmed and washed

For the orange dressing:

1 teaspoon (5 ml spoon) French mustard

2 tablespoons (2 × 15 ml spoon) orange juice

grated rind of 1 orange

4 fl oz (110 ml) olive oil

sea salt

Definitely treat-time: cashews are a terrific price so this is a real luxury salad, but one worth taking out a mortgage for!

Mix all the salad ingredients together.

Combine the mustard and orange juice, mix to a smooth paste and stir in the orange rind. Slowly stir in the olive oil so that the sauce is well-blended and season to taste with the sea salt. Toss the salad with the dressing just before serving.

FRENCH BEANS VINAIGRETTE POIVRE-VERT

Preparation time 15 minutes + standing Serves 4

1 lb (450 g) french beans

1 teaspoon (5 ml spoon) French mustard

1 tablespoon (15 ml spoon) white wine vinegar

4 fl oz (110 ml) olive oil

2 teaspoons (2 × 5 ml spoon) green peppercorns, crushed

salt and pepper

This vinaigrette, flavoured with crushed green peppercorns, transforms the simplest of salads into a gastronomic treat. It goes particularly well with lightly cooked french beans, and can be served as a side salad or even as a starter.

Cook the beans in a pan of boiling water until they are 'al dente', and cool. Mix the mustard with the vinegar and gradually stir in the oil. Season to taste with salt and pepper and finally stir in the crushed peppercorns. Leave to stand for at least half an hour before tossing with the beans.

Cashew Nut Salad with Orange Dressing
French Beans Vinaigrette Poivre-vert

MUSHROOM SALAD WITH GREEN PEPPER SAUCE

Preparation time 25 minutes + chilling — Serves 2–3

3 tablespoons (3 × 15 ml spoon) vegetable oil

6 oz (175 g) button mushrooms, sliced

For the sauce:

2 green peppers

2 large cloves of garlic, unpeeled

2 tablespoons (2 × 15 ml spoon) fresh fennel leaves, chopped

1 tablespoon (15 ml spoon) olive oil

The pepper sauce in this salad has a thick, creamy consistency, and the raw mushrooms remain firm yet soft underneath it. It is delicious.

Heat the oil in a frying pan and sauté the mushrooms very quickly. Drain and cool. Boil the peppers and garlic together for 6 minutes, then drain and pop the garlic out of its skin. Liquidise with the fennel and the oil and spoon over the mushrooms. Chill.

MUSHROOM AND PASTA SALAD

Preparation time 20 minutes + a few hours marinating — Serves 4

8 oz (225 g) pasta bows

8 oz (225 g) button mushrooms, sliced

1 large clove of garlic, crushed

½ pint (300 ml) natural yogurt

sea salt and black pepper

A simple combination, this, but exquisitely dressed with yogurt and flavoured with garlic. It goes with all kinds of main dishes, and is a wonderful buffet party piece.

Boil the pasta bows until 'al dente', drain and cool. Mix the pasta bows with the sliced mushrooms and put in a bowl. Add the garlic to the yogurt and season to taste with salt and freshly ground black pepper. Toss the pasta and mushrooms in the dressing and leave to marinate for several hours.

MEAL PLANNER

LUNCH PARTY MENUS

1 Potted Cheese with Herbs
Spinach Layers
Lemon Rice with Spinach, Artichokes Dijonnaise and a green salad
Fresh fruit salad with profiteroles

2 Garlic Soup
Asparagus Puffs
Herbed Cucumbers and Spicy Spinach Purée
Gooseberry fool

3 Leeks en Croûte with Mushroom Purée
Sesame Aubergines with Noodles
Sweetcorn Chinese Style, Artichokes à la Grecque and a green salad
Pineapple mousse

4 Sesame Wafers
Savoury Ratatouille Crumble
Potatoes Romanoff and Chicory and Fennel in Coriander Vinaigrette
Crème brulée

5 Crostini Fiorentini
Garlic Cheese Flan
Creamed Celery with Almonds, Courgettes in Spinach Sauce and a green salad
Chocolate soufflé

6 Corn Chowder
Cheese and Pimento Omelette Soufflé
Potatoes Gruyère and Deep-fried Cauliflower Masala
Rum baba and cream

7 Avocado Pâté
Saffron Risotto
Malay Cabbage and Courgette and Leek Salad with Blue Cheese Dressing
Grapefruit sorbet

8 Baked Eggs in Courgettes
Indonesian Rice Cakes
Beetroot with Yogurt and Hazelnuts, Tomato and Gherkin Salad with Yogurt and Shredded Leek Salad
Apfel strudel

9 Black Bean Soup
Risotto with Fennel and Petits Pois
Spiced Lentil Purée, papadoms and a green salad
Blackcurrant sorbet

10 Cold Spinach and Lentil Soup
Tiropitta with Spring Onion
Beetroot with Orange Sauce, Mixed Vegetable Salad with Peanut Sauce and a green salad
Apricot fool with meringues

11 Brie and Olive Squares
Shallot Soup with Cheese
Layered Vegetable Terrine
Spiced Lentil and Pineapple Salad and a green salad
Blackcurrant ice cream

12 Sesame Wafers
Chilled Walnut Soup
Garlic Cheese Flan
Cold Choucroute, Mushroom Salad with Green Pepper Sauce and Cold Stuffed Tomatoes
Peach sorbet

DINNER PARTY MENUS

1 Avocado and Roquefort Puffs
Layered Vegetable Terrine
Shredded Leek Salad, French Beans Vinaigrette Poivre-vert, Mushrooms Stuffed with Aubergine Purée, a green salad and Granary bread
Vacherin chantilly with Melba sauce

2 Corn Cobs Baked with Herb Butter
Aubergine Soufflé
Crunchy Sliced Potatoes, Baby Broad Beans with Poppy Seeds, Brussels Sprouts with Garlic and Parmesan and a green salad
Mint sorbet
Poire belle Helène

3 Cauliflower with Coriander Vinaigrette
Four-cheese Tagliatelle
Steamed Fennel with Light Ginger Sauce, Carrots with Garlic and Ginger and a green salad
Strawberry gâteau
Floating islands

4 Stilton and Walnut Bites
Florence Fennel Soup
Kedgeree with Summer Vegetables
Cabbage Masala, Cashew Nut Salad with Orange Dressing, papadoms and a green salad
Pears baked with macaroons
Praline ice cream

5 Tangy Avocado
Mild Lentil and Mixed Vegetable Curry
Spiced Lentil Purée, plain rice, papadoms and a lettuce and onion salad
Orange soufflé
Raspberry pavlova

6 Giant Stuffed Mushrooms
Jellied Tomato Ring
Lemon Rice Salad, Chicory and Fennel in Coriander Vinaigrette, Courgette and Leek Salad with Blue Cheese Dressing and garlic bread
Linzer torte
Apple charlotte and cream

7 Creamy Olive Pâté
Stuffed Courgettes with Red Pepper Sauce
Bright Bean Salad, Mushroom and Pasta Salad, Meaux Potato Salad and a tomato salad with onion rings
Hazelnut meringue gâteau

8 Cheese and Leek Soufflé Vol-au-vents
Penne with Peppers
Courgettes with Mace and Cream, Stir-fried Cabbage with Mushrooms and Beansprouts, papadoms and a green salad
Caramel oranges
Lemon mousse

9 White Bean and Chick-pea Salad
Okra and Courgettes in Lentil Sauce
Potatoes in Garlic and Parsley Butter, Cumin Cauliflower and a green salad
Bavarois a l'orange
Lemon and almond tart

10 Fried Indian Mix
Cold Three-coloured Pepper Soup
Black-eyed Beanfeast
Spiced Okra, Chunky Spiced Corn Cobs, papadoms and a green salad
Crème caramel
Coffee meringue cake

11 Dreamy Dip
Aubergines Provençale
Noodles Oriental Style
Chinese Leaves with Juniper, Baked Onion with Cumin Seeds and a tomato salad
Strawberry gâteau
Fresh fruit salad with profiteroles

12 Crispy-fried Chick-peas
Rolled Sorrel Pancakes
Okra and Courgettes in Lentil Sauce
Timbale of Mushrooms, Sweet Pepper Purée, rice and a green salad
Black cherry cheesecake

13 Melon Spears
Courgette Soufflé Crêpes
Leek Tian
Petits Pois with Fennel, French Beans Vinaigrette Poivre-vert and a green salad
Pears in red wine
Apricot flan

INDEX TO RECIPES

Design and layout: Ken Vail Graphic Design
Photography: Andrew Whittuck
Stylist: Marie O'Hara
The publishers wish to thank Dickins and Jones, Regent Street, London W1, for the loan of some of the items which appear in the photographs of this book.
Food preparation for photography: Liz & Pete
Illustrations: Mandy Doyle
Typesetting: Hands Fotoset, Leicester
Printed and bound by Balding & Mansell Ltd, Wisbech, Cambs